# THE WORKERS' EDUCATIONAL
## ASSOCIATION

# THE WORKERS'
# EDUCATIONAL
# ASSOCIATION

## THE FIRST FIFTY YEARS

by Mary Stocks

George Allen & Unwin Ltd

RUSKIN HOUSE MUSEUM STREET LONDON

First Published 1953

Reprinted 1968 by Cedric Chivers Ltd., Bath,
at the request of The Library Association,
ECM - ANTON HAIN K.G.
Printed in Germany

# PREFACE

THE W.E.A. has, during its fifty years of existence, comprised a mass of activities, individual and corporate, up and down the United Kingdom and over the seas. These activities have been carried on by thousands of keen workers—some prominent, others obscure. In the course of writing the history of these years I have read innumerable reports and talked to a number of people—some of them with memories much longer than my own—whose help has been invaluable. Whether the resulting chronicle of events will strike them as reasonably competent or quite the reverse I do not know. But this I do know. Everyone who reads it will be conscious of its omissions. Somebody whose work should have been mentioned has been passed over. Some phase of W.E.A. activity which should have been brought into the picture has been left out of it. Some development which should have had a chapter to itself has been squeezed into a paragraph. In saying this I am not trying to disarm criticism of my sense of literary proportion, or my acumen in selecting the right material from the mass that is available. I am sure that I deserve criticism on both counts. But I do ask my comrades in the W.E.A. to accord a measure of sympathy to an author confronted with so much interesting material, so many records of branch and district enterprise, such rich chronicles of individual initiative and devotion—in face of an austere determination to produce a book small enough to be marketed at a reasonable price.

MARY STOCKS

# CONTENTS

PREFACE                                        *page* 5

Chapter

1   Nineteen Three                               9

2   Albert Mansbridge                           19

3   Infancy of the W.E.A.                       27

4   Evolution of the Tutorial Class            37

5   The W.E.A. Grows Up                         48

6   World War Number One                        64

7   The Struggle for the Trade
    Unions                                      80

8   The W.E.A. Looks at Itself                 103

9   World War Number Two                       120

10  The Post-War Years                         139

# CHAPTER ONE

# NINETEEN THREE

THERE is at first sight no very spectacular significance about the year 1903 except that the Workers' Educational Association happened to be born in it. It is therefore relevant to the story of this body, to note certain features of that otherwise insignificant year. In tracing the fortunes of the W.E.A. through the succeeding half-century it will be seen that the aims of its leaders, and for that matter their methods, were largely conditioned by the social environment in which they started their work at the turn of the century and by the changes which have since transformed the social structure of England: its appearance, its class-composition, the factors which shape and the ideas which inspire its politics, and the material requirements which direct its economic endeavour. These changes, acting and reacting on one another, have been spectacular, potent and profound. Indeed, it would be true to say that the fifty years of the W.E.A.'s existence cover a Social Revolution which will provide future historians with as concise a chapter-heading as the Industrial Revolution of a century earlier. It is, then, against this background of England in transition that we must envisage the expanding activities of the W.E.A. and it will remain for readers of its story to estimate its ability to adapt itself to these changes as well as the degree of its responsibility for their occurrence.

In 1903 Queen Victoria was dead, but she had been so long alive that it still seemed a little odd to talk about King's Counsellors or His Majesty's Theatre—or, for that matter, to sing "God Save the King". The South African War had been fought and won but it was still "*The* War" in common speech. It seemed to many who contemplated with distaste the political operations which initiated it and the military operations which characterized it, that national self-respect might yet be restored by the wise and generous handling of a defeated enemy. Though a Conservative Government still occupied the seat of power, and Liberalism in the shape of a powerfully organized political party with unusually gifted leaders was still three years short of its golden opportunity, liberalism as a political philosophy was widespread and deep-rooted. It was, in fact, what the Church had been in past centuries: the unifying force of Western civilization. Where it had no significant existence, as for instance in Czarist Russia, it would inevitably and in due course come to birth.

Fresh in men's memories was a horrible affair in France: the Dreyfus case. That a man should suffer gross injustice because he happened to be a Jew, and this in a land so near that one could see it on a clear day from the English coast, was indeed a solemn thought. Human progress, it seemed, had still far to go. It might, indeed, take a long time to reach whatever millennium was envisaged by reasonable liberal-minded people. It might crawl in bottom gear—the simile is, of course, a gross anachronism—or speed in top. It might even pause in neutral. But the car of progress had no reverse. So one would tacitly assume that such goings-on as banditry, outlawry, gun-running or massacre were the stuff of romantic literature or of tales told about South American Republics. The Psalms, with their conception of captive nations and mass exile, expressed emotions which civilized mortals no longer had occasion to feel, and thus offered consolations of which our age had no need. Their relevance to twentieth-century religious experience was often in question.

Meanwhile, so rationally serene was the relation of sovereign states to one another in this well-ordered and steadily progressive world that *The Times Atlas* was issued in imperishable leather binding as a reference book which, like the family Bible, would require no periodic revision. And anybody who wished to take a holiday abroad had only to look up trains in the *Continental Bradshaw*, change his English gold at a minutely fluctuating rate of exchange, and to the amount required, into whatever currency he fancied, take a ticket, and start off. There were certain lawless areas of the earth's surface where it might be desirable to travel with a British passport, but one did not normally regard them as holiday resorts but rather as fields for adventurous exploration. Thus, at the outset of any holiday season one could observe travellers converging by hansom, four-wheeler, brougham, victoria, landau or station 'bus on those London termini which led to the coast. One could also observe, though one would scarcely trouble to do so, that these travellers were all, as demonstrated by their dress and the nature of their luggage, of the well-to-do class. There were not enough of them to produce queues at booking offices or "standing room only" in corridor trains—which contributed to the amenities of long-distance travel even when this led to home holiday haunts. And the haunts thus visited still had a quiet seemliness of their own. They were unpolluted by kiosks and camping grounds. Their retailers were not demoralized by seasonal pressures. Their landladies relied on the patronage of families whose members enjoyed space and relied on paid domestic service.

There were, however, alternative forms of holiday making. For those other than the well-to-do class—and these constituted some two-thirds of the population—periods of relaxation were brief. These would be marked by the bank-holiday week-ends, and in the north by the wakes weeks. But because they were brief so, too, were the journeys of those who enjoyed them. The day trip was as much as many could accomplish, and certain holiday resorts at no great distance from populous working-class areas catered for the "tripper". In fact this teeming company of the non-privileged was by modern standards immobile. Where they worked there they stayed, and where they stayed there they took up, in proportion to their numbers, comparatively little space. There is, perhaps, nothing which so conduces to the sense of being a privileged class as the ability to move about while other people stay put. This was an outstanding feature of the class-structure of England in the year 1903.

It was not the only feature. There was also the sense, enjoyed by the well-to-do, of being buoyed up on what can be described as a comfortable cushion of paid domestic service. This was reflected in the structure of domestic architecture. In London it had long since produced the familiar pattern of urban terraces with working quarters for the domestic staff in the basement and sleeping quarters in the attics. Houses thus constructed were still largely occupied by single families in the manner for which they were originally intended. Outside London the pattern was more varied and the domestic expansiveness of the well-to-do took horizontal rather than vertical forms. All this meant that the day-to-day experiences of the well-to-do differed profoundly from those of the weekly wage-earners, and this was especially true in respect of their wives, whose incursions into the kitchen involved nothing more strenuous than the giving out of stores and the dictating of menus.

The origins of this clearly defined class structure lay far back in history and deep in the interstices of the economic system—or rather absence of system—and certain factors had been continuously in operation to hold the form of this stratification in place. Of these, one of the most potent was an educational system which operated as both cause and effect of inequality of income. Its main features were roughly as follows:—

Among the well-to-do it was the common practice to send both boys and girls to a privately run day school until the age of about nine years. Alternatively, a home governess might be employed where a suitable day school was not within easy distance. At the age of nine, or thereabouts, the boys would be dispatched to a privately run preparatory boarding school. This breach in the family circle often occasioned acute misery to both parents and child, but it was regarded as necessary that the young male should be subjected to the discipline and routine of exile. The girls were usually allowed to remain at home and the Girls' Public Day School Trust provided a series of excellent high schools in middle-class areas. At twelve or thirteen the boys would be transferred to one or other of a group of "public schools" in which the educational regime was of first-rate quality. These schools, with inherited traditions of academic excellence, attracted some of the best talent in the teaching profession. Operating through small classes, they certainly produced educational value for the very large sums required of their patrons. From the public schools, boys would proceed at the age of eighteen or nineteen to one of the ancient universities or into some form of professional training which would, in due course, offer the economic opportunity to reproduce this educational pattern in their own offspring. For lower-salaried professional men the endowed grammar schools offered opportunities for day-school education of no less distinguished academic quality, though lacking the social status of the "public" boarding schools. The non-resident civic universities of nineteenth-century origin also offered opportunities for higher education to those unable to afford existence at Oxford or Cambridge.

For the great mass of the working classes the educational pilgrimage was simpler and shorter. Education consisted of eight years at a free elementary school maintained by the Education Committee of the local County or County Borough Council. These schools, which the Balfour Education Act of the preceding year had transferred from the School Boards instituted in 1870 and from the religious bodies which had provided and maintained schools of recognized standard, still for the most part occupied their ancient buildings. They were still, by force of habit, referred to as "board schools" and the certificated, or in some cases non-certificated non-graduates who taught in them, were referred to as "teachers" in contrast to the "schoolmasters" and "schoolmistresses" of the schools supplying more advanced education. From these newly constituted council elementary schools the overwhelming majority of children proceeded at the age of thirteen to wage-earning occupations and their curriculum was conditioned by the assumption that they would in fact do so. There had been, however, from time immemorial a tenuous "educational ladder" by which exceptionally brilliant children with exceptionally enlightened and self-sacrificing parents could climb, by means of competitive scholarships, from the elementary to the grammar school, and from there to the university. This possibility had by 1903 been appreciably widened by a section of the Balfour Education Act which empowered the new Local Education Authorities to provide rate-aided secondary schools. The red light which the Cockerton Judgment of 1900 had shown to those School Boards which had ventured to spend public money on secondary education had thus changed to green. There was no requirement so to act, but there was permission, and of that permission the more progressive education authorities availed themselves with varying degrees of generosity. The rate-aided municipal secondary school was coming into the picture. It was a feature of the utmost significance.

The economic implications of this educational dichotomy are immediately obvious. By confining the opportunities for secondary and higher education to a relatively small section of the community, it enabled those who enjoyed such opportunities to compete for the better-paid and more responsible occupations requiring such an educational background, within a sort of ring fence—shielded from the rivalry of the excluded majority with its potential but untapped competitive ability. Thus the higher income levels, and the professional standards of domestic life and culture associated with them, were preserved and handed on from generation to generation. The few who succeeded in climbing the "educational ladder", and the rather larger number who by exceptional business enterprise, or luck, were able to exploit the opportunities of a free-price economy sufficiently to secure expensive educational opportunities for their sons made little perceptible difference to the class-pattern of England in the year 1903. They did, however, contribute an element of fluidity, and their existence provided a spectacular incentive.

Karl Marx has pointed out that every social system carries within itself the germs of its own destruction. There were many such germs operating on the vitals of England's social system in 1903. Of these, one of the most potent, though its existence is scarcely illustrative of the Marxian formula, was the reforming zeal of those members of the privileged classes whose consciences rejected privilege. They had already made their mark in the sphere of education and were notably active on the London County Council. How far their activities represented a far-sighted conscious attempt to undermine the class basis of society and batter a way for the under-privileged into the ring fence of economic opportunity it is difficult to say. Many of them were prepared to accept the implications of what they were doing, and some were openly subversive of the familiar class pattern. There was, however, a widespread belief that the great heritage of human culture, its art, drama, music, literature and scholarship, should be shared by all; and that the apathy of those who appeared not to desire a share was conditioned by harsh environment and blunted sensitivity. It was this missionary zeal on behalf of culture which had rallied an active band of well-to-do voluntary workers to the settlement movement initiated by Canon Barnett at Toynbee Hall in East London. It was this same missionary zeal which a generation earlier had inspired F. D. Maurice and F. J. Furnivall to establish a Working Men's College, and at the turn of the century two well-to-do Americans had established a residential working-men's college under the name of Ruskin Hall in Oxford. The same missionary zeal had carried university teachers outside the walls of their universities as far back as the eighteen seventies, to meet through University Extension Lectures, the needs of those who were conscious of a desire for intellectual riches which fate, or fortune, or geographical isolation had denied them. "Freely ye have received, freely give" might have served as their biblical text had they required one.

It was Cambridge University that made the first move in the University Extension adventure, as far back as 1873. Oxford followed in 1876. The newer universities already had ways of their own for carrying education outside the walls, but these in due course were approximated to the pattern of University Extension Departments constituted for the purpose of providing courses in response to local demand. The demand was undoubtedly there, but it was not unconnected with certain features of the class-structure already described. The lightly taxed incomes of the well-to-do classes and the relatively inexpensive domestic service which they could command, ensured the existence of a considerable class of leisured women: wives and unmarried daughters. These women were as well educated as their husbands and brothers—less systematically perhaps, but what they lacked in classics and mathematics they often made up in modern languages and the wider culture which they absorbed by living at home and conversing with mature and cultivated people. It was very largely from the ranks of such women that the settlement residents, club-workers, poor-law guardians and active social reformers of the late Victorian and Edwardian age were drawn. And University Extension offered them alternative or additional opportunities for quenching their intellectual thirst. Up and down the country they formed groups of intelligent responsive adult students who could afford to pay the fairly substantial fees required to finance a course of extension lectures which would, as often as not, be given during the early afternoon. But that was not the whole story of University Extension, nor were the efforts of the rich to civilize the poor the only springs of what we have learned to call the Adult Education Movement.

The Son of Sirach, who was no less famous than Solomon for wisdom among the ancient Hebrews, knew as much as we know today about the impediments to culture presented by continuous manual labour. He reminds us in the Book of Ecclesiasticus, that "the wisdom of a learned man cometh by opportunity of leisure". And how, he asks, "shall *he* get wisdom that holdeth the plough"? The ploughman, the cowman, the carpenter, the metal-worker and the potter—these "maintain the state of the world" and "without these cannot a city be inhabited". But "they shall not dwell where they will nor go up and down: they shall not be sought for in public counsel, nor sit high in the congregation: they shall not sit in the judge's seat, nor understand the sentence of judgment". It must not be assumed that he was satisfied with this state of affairs. Indeed, he associated it with a state of class-warfare in which "as the wild ass is the lion's prey in the wilderness: so the rich eat up the poor". Later writers have not described the class struggle more forcibly though they have done so at greater length. But the position defined by the Son of Sirach in the second century B.C. was perfectly apprehended and increasingly resented by the wage-earners of England as they emerged from the industrial revolution in the early decades of the nineteenth century with a new corporate sense of economic, political and cultural deprivation. By the time we come to 1903 the Labour Representation Committee with four Labour M.P.s were building the foundations of what three years later was to be known as the Labour Party. Some million and a half trade unionists were vigorously upholding the wage-earner's claim to a share in the expanding productivity of a still expanding free-price economy. But both the political and industrial wings of this clearly defined Labour Movement were heavily preoccupied with the implications of the Taff Vale judgment which two years earlier had put trade-union finances at the mercy of legal actions for damages. So much energy was directed to the legislative redress of an intolerable situation that little was left for general educational activities. It was from a less preoccupied section of the wage-earning class that the really constructive drive for educational activity came—or rather from wage-earners organized for other than political or defensive purposes.

From its earliest days the Consumers' Co-operative Movement had been interested in education. Education was one of the professed aims of the movement and many co-operative societies lived up to their profession of faith. The economics and social ethics of co-operation in themselves offered a wide and relevant field of study for co-operative members. But the co-operative societies did not stop at that. Many of them anticipated the spread of public libraries by providing books and reading-rooms for their members. Many of them appointed education committees to keep the educational pot boiling.

To the Co-operative Movement extension lectures offered a golden opportunity of bringing their more educationally minded members into touch with teachers of university standing. The societies could offer scholarships to selected members to attend Extension Summer Meetings in Oxford or Cambridge. They could provide serious groups of students for courses in particular localities. They could press for lectures at hours when working-class students would be free to attend: And for many of the extension lecturers themselves such students and such group contacts offered a new inspiration and stimulus. It is recorded[1] that "Mr. Hudson Shaw, the most prominent of University Extension Lecturers, so far as working men and women were concerned, deemed it almost a *sine qua non* to have the assistance of the local Co-operative Societies in industrial centres, if his work was to succeed."

It is obvious, therefore, that in the class-ridden free-price economy of 1903 England, there was quite a lot of adult education going on—very much more, indeed, than is chronicled here. In co-operative societies and university extra-mural departments, in adult schools and clubs, in working men's

[1] *An Adventure in Working Class Education*, by Albert Mansbridge, p. 9.

colleges and philanthropic settlements and innumerable spontaneous groups which defy classification, workers who had left school at thirteen or fourteen with an unquenched intellectual thirst, restless middle-class women whose normal environment provided inadequate stimulus for the intellectual qualities they possessed, potential working-class leaders conscious that education was a key to power, and missionary scholars, who, believing that what they had was good, wished that others should have it—all these were working away with enthusiasm and hope. But they were working unsystematically and often in isolation from one another. T. W. Price has summed the matter up in his history of the W.E.A.'s first twenty-one years, in words which cannot be improved on. "The result of the operations of all these agencies was less to create a movement than to set up a *ferment*." But in the heart of this ferment and contributing significantly to its effervescence, was the man who, more than any other man, was responsible for transforming the ferment into a movement. He was an employee of the Co-operative Wholesale Society, and his name was Albert Mansbridge.

# CHAPTER TWO

# ALBERT MANSBRIDGE

ALBERT MANSBRIDGE was born at Gloucester in the year 1876, the son of a carpenter. At the age of three he attended a neighbouring dame school, the fee for which was a pot of jam. At the age of four he entered the local Church school at which his only recorded memory is of severe admonition for having bitten a fellow pupil. In 1880 his family moved to London and the following year found them settled in Battersea. There he grew up.

It was, doubtless, this early migration which produced that characteristically Mansbridge accent which would have offered interesting scope to the phonetician hero of Shaw's play *Pygmalion*. It appeared, to the phonetically uninitiated, to be something in the nature of a cockney intonation superimposed on a west-country burr. Whether its unquestioned effectiveness as demonstrated in conversation, conference, pulpit or platform was due to its aesthetic cadence or to the personality which it expressed must be left an open question. It was, however, peculiarly Mansbridge, and its almost hypnotic potency as an instrument of persuasion is beyond doubt.

The significant phase of Mansbridge's education: the point at which he deviated from the beaten highway leading from board school to wage-earning, came at the age of ten when, having reached the sixth standard which represented the board school's educational ceiling, he gained a scholarship to the Sir Walter St. John's Middle School, and another two years later to the Battersea Grammar School. This disentanglement from the set pattern of proletarian education brought him new contacts with families of the professional class as well as a wider and more stimulating curriculum. It brought him little else, because domestic finances prevented him from remaining at school after fourteen to compete for the Oxford or Cambridge scholarship which his school record indicated as a brilliant possibility. But as things were, he found for himself the intellectual and cultural outlets for which his soul craved. Museums and picture galleries, churches and the sermons preached in them by eminent theologians, Bible study, political meetings, London parks and visits to Gloucestershire relatives, the flow of the Thames past Battersea on its majestic journey through the heart of London to the sea—all that he heard and saw and read went to feed his insatiable intellectual appetite, an appetite that grows with what it feeds on. But at no point does he appear to have drawn the conclusion that sedulous cultivation of these liberating influences might lead to his emergence from the proletarian rut into some stratosphere of individual social eminence. His interest lay in the elimination of the rut. What he found good others must have. The windows through which he viewed the great expanse of human experience must be open to all. If people preferred them shut, that was because they did not know what kind of a landscape they opened up. They must be shown. He was, and indeed remained throughout his life, a very religious man, and it was part of his religion to bring to others that more abundant life which he himself found good. But he would have done it in any case; he was that sort of man.

If he had been born in the year 1934, the opportunities presented by the 1944 Education Act, plus the financial benefits of the "Welfare State" would undoubtedly have opened a way for him to Oxford or Cambridge. As it was, family finances having required him to leave school at fourteen, he became junior clerk—he preferred the more realistic description of "office boy"—to a city firm of guano merchants at a wage of 7s. 6d. a week. A year later he became a boy copyist in a government department—a civil servant in fact—and had not so far to go to work. Time saved was time available for educational activities. He attended evening lectures at the Battersea Polytechnic; he founded and edited magazines; he sustained the Band of Hope; he taught in Sunday School; since Westminster was his lunch-hour playground, he absorbed between bouts of copying and filing, the history, architecture and ritual of Westminster Abbey which became, he says, his university.

A photograph dated 1894 shows an earnest and immaculately

groomed youth clad in the white surplice of a licensed lay reader. This was the year in which a significant encounter occurred which is best told in his own words[1] :—

> While I was editing the paper [a magazine run in connection with the Junior Civil Service Prayer Union] Charles Gore was delivering his famous course of Lent lectures in Westminster Abbey, expounding the Sermon on the Mount. I was so impressed that I wrote boldly asking him for an article. He declined to write it, but asked me to visit him. One Friday evening in June 1894, I called timorously at his house in the Little Cloisters. His welcome was inexpressibly beautiful. My imagination had never before conceived so high a type of man. He asked me to stay to supper. At it I met his fellow members of the Community of the Resurrection, which he had founded, and other guests. In such a way I entered for the first time the big world. Clumsy and shy as I was, yet I was encouraged to talk, and soon did so freely. As I listened, however, I remember realizing for the first time that the newspapers were not to be relied on as records of actual happenings. These men knew, and as they talked of incidents and scenes, not only in the House of Commons, but in many important institutions and places, I gained new views of life and manners.

In his great poem, *Biography*, John Masefield reminds us that the external records of a human life may tell us little of its supremely significant moments. It may tell the wrong story, fail to tell the whole story, or tell the right story wrongly emphasized. And so the importance of some chance encounter leading indirectly to a change of direction may elude recognition. What is true of biography is less true of history where mass movements play a larger part and chance meetings a lesser part—perhaps, indeed, no significant part at all. So those who write history must resist the temptation to dramatize particular incidents and thus understress the wide or remote causes against whose background they occur. It would be good "theatre" but bad history to dramatize this encounter between the boy copyist and the eminent scholar—accepting and exaggerating Mansbridge's own estimate of its personal significance—and presenting it as the curtain to Act I or the opening incident of Act II in the drama of his life's work. There is, however, a lesser temptation which it is impossible to resist, and that is to indicate it as symbolic of a partnership which gave direction to Mansbridge's ideas about working-class

[1] *The Trodden Road*, by Albert Mansbridge, p. 28.

education, which became the characteristic feature of the movement which he founded, and which has been accepted by its leading men and women as the basis of its policy through the half-century of its existence. It is the partnership between enlightened scholarship and working-class aspiration.

There is a strain of unreason in the attitude of those who, while recognizing that the privileged classes have done well for themselves in the matter of education and exercised power by virtue of it, are nevertheless prepared to repudiate the scholarship of the ages kept alive by the universities as not worth having. Whether they know it or not they are responding all too readily to our latter-day glorification of the "common man" with its denegration of "mere scholarship" and its use of the word "academic" to indicate that which is useless or unreal. It is certainly true that the well-to-do critic of education who sings praises to "craftsmanship" and denegrates "book-learning" has no intention whatever of withdrawing his own son from school at the age of fifteen and apprenticing him to a craft. His attitude, whether he knows it or not, is that the wider culture is good for the few but if too many acquire it the few are unlikely to have such a pleasant time. It is, however, no less true, and no less true than it was in the days of the Son of Sirach, that manual workers are the pillars of society, that they "maintain the state of the world" and that "without these cannot a city be inhabited". One cannot, at our present stage of productive technique, contemplate a world in which some large group of persons does not function as manual workers. At the same time, one would not or should not wish to contemplate a world in which they are assigned to their role by the economic weakness of their parents or robbed of their share of the kingdom of the mind. Mansbridge the under-privileged, and Gore the over-privileged, found themselves in perfect agreement on this point in the year 1894.

As far as Mansbridge was concerned an equally, if not more significant contact followed close on the heels of his newly acquired friendship with Gore. In the following year he became engaged to Frances Jane Pringle, a fellow Sunday School teacher, at his local church. Fate was indeed kind to him. Having supplied the social contacts he needed, it added the perfect permanent working partner for the work he had to do. All this made him very happy. And his happiness made him so much the more an effective missioner for the culture he was acquiring himself and persuading others to desire.

It was from the platform of the Consumers' Co-operative Movement that he made his first important move. The economics of this movement, fortified by Gore's interest in it, satisfied his Christian social conscience, and he found its personnel to be on the whole education-conscious. In 1896 he entered its service as clerk in the tea department of the Co-operative Wholesale Society's warehouse in Whitechapel. There, though the work was monotonous and offered little prospect of advancement, he was able to develop his spare-time interests, both as learner and teacher, within the framework of the movement which he served. And, indeed, outside it—for in 1898 he was accepted as a typewriting and social history instructor in one of the London School Board's evening commercial schools. Later we find him functioning as delegate, with a known enthusiasm for education, at successive co-operative conferences. Of course he never was—never could be—satisfied with the teaching supplied by the Co-operative Movement from its own limited resources of teaching experience and intellectual range. He had himself tapped the springs of learning at university level—so for that matter had the Co-operative Movement in so far as it already made use of University Extension. But in Mansbridge's view it was necessary that the Co-operative Movement should draw upon these springs much more heavily: much more systematically. His opportunity to say so came in 1898 when he attended a Whit week-end Co-operative Congress at Peterborough. As a result he was invited to read a paper on "Co-operation and Education in Citizenship" at a conference of co-operators held in connection with the Oxford University Extension Summer meeting in 1899.

The result was somewhat discouraging. Many co-operators felt that their movement was already doing a lot in the educational line, and doing it quite well. His paper was coldly received. But that did not put him out of heart with his thesis. It caused him, rather, to elaborate it. It was not enough, he argued, for the workers to provide ready-made audiences for university lecturers. They must have some say in the quality and direction of the education provided. Nor was it enough to base the working-class side of the partnership on the Co-operative Movement. The trade unions must be brought into the picture.

Mansbridge was not, of course, the only educational enthusiast at work on the partnership idea. On the other side there was John Holland Rose, later recognized as a leading political historian, but at this early date one of the most popular of extension lecturers and editor of the *University Extension Journal*. He, too, was conscious of the need for more constructive thought on adult education. Accordingly, he invited Mansbridge to air his views in his *Journal* and in January 1903 Mansbridge appeared in print. He contributed altogether three articles embodying a plan which had been taking shape in his mind since the cool reception of his speech in the summer of 1899.

Democracy, he argued in the first article, was suffering from "a hard veneer" imposed by elementary education which promotes the unthinking absorption of facts and renders men susceptible to mere rhetoric. Working men wish to act politically on governing bodies—lack of thinking power prevents them from doing so effectively. "Co-operation and trade unionism are the chief movements of democracy. University Extension, of all educational movements, promises most to be capable of infusing them with a wise and free education." He followed this up with an appeal to trade unionists to come into line with the Co-operative Movement in a full realization of the "glory of education". He pointed out that in spite of setbacks University Extension had already "secured a definite stand upon the educational basis of co-operation", and ended with an appeal to the University Extension Movement "to settle itself deliberately upon trade unionism and co-operation, where, in spite of opposition and dead days, it will finally see the day of fruition and be satisfied".

In his second article he came down to earth with the title "A Plan of Action". He referred more fully to the qualifications of the Extension and Co-operative Movements in respect of working-class education and to the measure of success already achieved by their working alliance. He indicated that more could be done by the appointment of co-operators and trade unionists to act as secretaries or co-secretaries where such working alliance was already operative. The duty of these secretaries would be the organization of groups of working men with a view to their inclusion in the University Extension Centre. They might even promote and sustain a centre. This organized and officially recognized participation should be the basis of grant-aid by the local co-operative society. But in due course it should be something more. To quote Mansbridge's own words: "This organization proceeding quietly would be ultimately controlled, if constitutionally possible, by a joint committee of university extensionists, co-operators, and trade unionists; which joint committee would subordinate to itself, or exercise some control over, the various local committees founded upon the same plan. The procedure of trade unionists, in order to secure the requisite official recognition by their trade union, would necessarily be more protracted than that of co-operators, because trade unionism has no educational machinery, as such, in existence." He concludes by facing the major obstacle: "an unpardonable suspicion of the university, on the part of leading co-operators, often flavoured with contempt, and a pronounced antipathy to anything that can possibly be misconstrued into a desire on the part of any movement, educational or otherwise, pushing its own educational work, to exploit them". He observed, however, a recognition on the part of the more progressive younger men "that it does not matter who educates, provided the education is real", and concluded with an impassioned reference to the "deep draughts of knowledge" which will "divert the strong movements of the people from the narrow paths of immediate interests to the broad way of that rightly ordered social life of which only glimpses have yet been seen even by the greatest of the world's seers".

In the third article, entitled "An Association", he discussed the relationship of such an organization to the three specified movements, and the composition of its executive committee. This should comprise representatives of the four existing University Extension Departments as well as co-operators and trade unionists: "in effect a joint committee". But, he admitted, "the ultimate constitutional relationship will, of necessity, depend upon the degree of constructive influence which can be brought to bear upon trade unionism in the future". In order to test the proposals he called for the initiation of a "pioneer association".

Holland Rose was enthusiastically in favour of proceeding with the plan. Canon Barnett of Toynbee Hall, to whom one would naturally go with any projected scheme for the betterment of working-class conditions, was less so. He said it would need a lot of money—£50,000 perhaps. Mrs. Mansbridge produced a lower estimate. She thought it could be done—for a start—on 2s. 6d., and this she was prepared to contribute from the Mansbridge housekeeping account. Accordingly, on Mansbridge's return from his discouraging encounter with Canon Barnett, an "Association to Promote the Higher Education of Working Men" was duly constituted with an operating capital of 2s. 6d. Its name was longer than its membership, which consisted of Albert and Frances Mansbridge. The former was unanimously elected honorary secretary by the latter. The Association was in being. In due course its name contracted and its membership grew.

# CHAPTER THREE

# INFANCY OF THE W.E.A.

FOR an organization which started its existence with a 50 per cent female membership, its name was lacking in descriptive accuracy and redolent of masculine arrogance. This defect was wholly unintentional and was remedied in 1905 when nine words were reduced to three and the Mansbridge organization became known to the world as the Workers' Educational Association: W.E.A. to its closer intimates. So far, this story of its birth has brought into our orbit only Mansbridge and Mrs. Mansbridge from the workers' side, Holland Rose and Gore from the universities. There was, of course, a much larger circle presiding at its birth. Having, so to speak, delivered the infant association, Mansbridge hastened to form a provisional committee from the ranks of known sympathizers in the trade union and co-operative movements. It comprised A. H. Thomas (brushmaker), George Alcock (railwayman), W. R. Salter (engineer), L. Idle and J. W. Cole (co-operative employees), with Mansbridge himself acting as honorary secretary. It met for the first time on July 14th, 1903, at Toynbee Hall, whose Warden, Canon Barnett, was delighted to note the falsification of his earlier pessimism and anxious to do all in his power to prove himself wrong.

Meanwhile, the other side had also made its first move. Dr. Holland Rose was busily preparing for publication in pamphlet form the three articles by Mansbridge which had set the ball rolling. "On behalf of the Education Committee of my brother lecturers", he wrote in an introduction to the reprint, "I would assure those to whom Mr. Mansbridge especially appeals that we are most anxious to make our movement as helpful as possible to them. The spirit that animated Charles Kingsley and Arnold Toynbee has never been more active at our ancient universities than it is today; and the time seems ripe for an educational advance on the lines here suggested." The "lines here suggested" were even more precisely defined on the inside cover of the pamphlet, where it was stated that an Association was in course of formation (April 1903), that its constitution would be determined and its officials elected at a meeting to be held in Oxford on the last Saturday of the Extension Summer Meeting, e.g. August 22nd, at 3 p.m., that individuals and societies were eligible for membership, that an annual subscription (subject to confirmation) of one shilling, together with "necessary donations" (italicized) would provide the funds of the Association, and that its honorary secretary (*pro tem.*) was Albert Mansbridge, of 52 Winsham Grove, West Side, Clapham Common. Such was the W.E.A.'s first publication.

The next step was to bring the two sides together. This was accomplished at the August conference foreshadowed in the pamphlet. It may go down to history as the inaugural meeting of the W.E.A. The extension secretaries of Oxford and Cambridge were active in support of it. Dr. Percival, Bishop of Hereford, and Dr. Kitchin, Dean of Durham, took turns at its chairmanship. R. Halstead, secretary of the Co-operative Productive Federation, was its leading speaker. Co-operators, trade unionists and university dons testified with one voice to the need for what Mansbridge described as "a strong and powerfully organized Association, so constructed as to be in distinct and immediate relationship, equally with the universities as with the working-class movements". The Association had a dignified send-off, being entertained to lunch in the Great Hall of St. John's College—at that time a stronghold of solid Oxford conservatism. But the host on this occasion was the senior tutor, Sidney Ball, a notable deviationist from his college traditions and an active member of the Fabian Society who was alleged, on insufficient evidence it must be admitted, to murmur "Religion and the Republic" when the college toast was "Church and King". It was certainly made clear during this summer week-end of 1903, that Holland Rose had spoken nothing but the truth when he asserted that the spirits of Kingsley and Toynbee were at large in the ancient universities. They were potent and ubiquitous.

The Association was by now well and truly launched and its committee, no longer "provisional", contained all the ingredients which Mansbridge had indicated as necessary for the concoction of his educational pie. Names notable in the academic world appear among its active supporters: Hudson Shaw, A. J. Carlyle, Joseph Owen, Professor H. H. Turner, A. L. Smith, Sir Oliver Lodge, Sir Alfred Dale, Sir Alfred Hopkinson, Professor J. H. B. Masterman. And among names notable in Labour circles we find W. J. Rowe, C. E. Wood, C. W. Bowerman, David Shackleton. Mansbridge had certainly got his ship buoyantly afloat on a good tide of progressive educational thought. Indeed it is difficult, looking back on this formative period, to determine how much of the ship's progress was due to wind and tide—how much to skilful navigation. Those who worked with Mansbridge at this time bear testimony to the infectious potency of his enthusiasm. He was aflame with what he called "the glory of education". He saw it like that, not at rhapsodical moments but all the time. And he could make other people see it like that. He could make other people do what he wanted them to do and he could make them think that it was what they themselves had always intended to do. They were all the more malleable because there was no positive reason why they should not do what he wanted; for apart from natural human apathy and some element of left-wing class prejudice against university lah-de-dah, there was as yet no constructive opposition to his plan for the development of university-cum-working-class education.

So Mansbridge, in all the spare time he could command, became the leading propagandist as well as the honorary secretary and treasurer of the new Association. His home—now transferred from Clapham Common to 198 Windsor Road, Ilford—was its office; his wife its secretarial staff. He visited co-operative societies and trade-union branches, as well as university dons who could be persuaded to undertake lectures or classes. He collected subscriptions; he promoted conferences. Following the example of the cuckoo, he took every opportunity of laying his propagandist eggs in other people's educational nests. But at the same time he enlarged and furnished his own. By the end of its first year the Association had 135 members and 11 affiliated co-operative societies; and its first Annual Report covering the period up to

June 30th, 1904, shows a subscription list of £42 18s. 6d. plus four guineas-worth of donations. Its income from all sources was £73 19s. 6d. and its expenses £63 3s. 10d., of which the major item was £10 for a typewriter, but nothing for salaries. Thus, Mansbridge completed his first year with a balance of £10 15s. 8d. and one valuable item of office equipment.

But that was not enough. Without branches the Association was as barren as a childless household. Branches were a vital part of the great idea. After all, the object of such an organization was to teach—not merely to talk about teaching; to organize the actual provision of working-class higher education, not merely to conduct propaganda in favour of its being provided. This provision must be organized locally among the people who were themselves desirous of receiving such education. It was work which could not be effectively done from the Mansbridges' parlour, even with the assistance of a £10 typewriter—or for that matter from a central London office with a paid secretarial staff, a private telephone switchboard and an electrically operated lift. Branches must be formed, and when formed, must reproduce the pattern of the Association at headquarters. They must embody that essential partnership between educational and working-class interests which was the essence of the great idea.

In October 1904 the first branch came into existence at Reading. The ground had been well prepared by Reading University College whose Principal, W. M. Childs, had already put considerable thought and energy into the development of extra-mural work. Reading was also fortunate in its Local Education Committee whose secretary, D. J. Pugh, was anxious to make vigorous use of the new powers conferred by the Act of 1902. It may be surmised that both the University College and the Local Education Committee were infused with the vigour of shining youth. Both were but two years old. Reading also boasted an exceptionally enlightened Co-operative Society whose education committee had been among the first eleven affiliates of Mansbridge's Association and whose members therefore knew precisely what was going on at number 198 Windsor Road, Ilford. But in his history of the W.E.A.'s first twenty-one years, T. W. Price suggests that whatever might have occurred or not occurred at headquarters, a permanent organization for adult education was well on the way in Reading by 1904—and as a Reading man by adoption, he should know. This illustrates the spontaneous character of the movement which Mansbridge was directing. Scholars and workers were making contact with one another all over the place. But as far as Reading enthusiasts were concerned, the knowledge that Mansbridge had formed a national association to promote the kind of work they themselves intended to do, suggested the possibility of useful outside contacts and more systematic procedure. And so—first came a representative conference comprising the familiar ingredients, then a branch with a governing body composed of representatives of affiliated local organizations with the Principal of the University College and the secretary of the Local Education Committee as *ex-officio* members. It was a model branch—and by the end of 1905 there were seven more.

This, of course, meant more work than ever for Mansbridge and in 1905 he resigned the job as cashier of the Co-operative Permanent Building Society, to which in 1901 he had transferred his allegiance from the C.W.S., and became full-time General Secretary of the Association at a starting salary of £50 a year. The increase, or for that matter the continuance, of this sum was on the knees of the gods—or rather on that of a small group of guarantors who had responded to a special appeal for enough money to support an office and a full-time secretary. At any rate, in 1905–6 we find an expenditure of £55 4s. on "salaries"; but the office was still the Mansbridge home, which by now contained a four-year-old son and was the scene of much educational hospitality: Mansbridge's own explanation of the economics of this remarkable *ménage* was that Mrs. Mansbridge was "a marvellous housekeeper". One can only assume that she knew how to administer five loaves and two fishes.

On August 12th, 1905, the W.E.A. met at Oxford for its first national conference, and in so doing took the field as a widely representative national organization to whose views on education the government in power might be expected to pay attention. A resolution was passed calling upon the Board of Education to cause Local Education Authorities to furnish information concerning the demand in their areas for compulsory attendance at evening continuation classes. From the conference a deputation went forth to the Board of Education, led by Will Crooks, and in due course the suggested inquiry was initiated. But it was nine years before any such idea was embodied in a statutory clause and a still-born clause it proved to be. A useful discussion was, however, set going. This gives the 1905 conference a limited historical importance. In another respect its importance is considerable, though this may not have been apparent at the time.

To it came a young Oxford don, a fellow of the Queen's College, named William Temple. Unlike Mansbridge he had been "born in the purple", the son of an archbishop married to the granddaughter of an earl. Lambeth Palace had been his home; Rugby and Balliol had provided his formal education. The philanthropic activities of school and university "missions" had provided such working-class contacts as he had. His position gave him access at high level to the world of learning and politics. His own intellectual power and inexhaustible energy, combined with a natural human geniality and a super-charge of Christian charity made him a significant and well-loved figure in whatever circle he graced and suggested to his contemporaries that a great future was in store for him. They were right. Don, headmaster, canon, bishop, archbishop, primate, his ascent to eminence was predictable and inevitable. It is seldom that the sons of eminent fathers escape being either enervated by what life offers them or discouraged by what it expects of them. William Temple escaped both dangers. It was not in him to be either enervated or discouraged.

At the moment with which we are now concerned, however, he had not so much as a "Rev." to his name. It was, Mansbridge records, "quite by chance" that he attended the W.E.A.'s first national conference; but it was by inclination, having found a cause after his own heart, that he became forthwith a member of the Association and in due course its first president. This, he said on a later occasion, was and was likely to remain, the greatest honour of his life. He did not, however, accept it as merely an honour, but rather as a responsible and at times arduous job, involving discussions of policy and all the niggling attendant work of drafting resolutions and attending committees, which an active chairman may shoulder and an inactive chairman leave to others. Many years later, after his retirement from the presidency under pressure of episcopal and archepiscopal duties, he had occasion to preside over a conference of adult education functionaries at Corpus Christi College, Oxford. It was one of his last activities before dying in harness. Few of those who took part in it were aware that their chairman spent his hard-earned lunch interval at a desk in Sir Richard Livingstone's study, drafting and redrafting a policy statement in response to the critical and hypercritical irresolution of his colleagues. It was an unforgettable demonstration of archespiscopal humility and human patience.

Among the considerations which turned his thoughts in the direction of Mansbridge's great idea was the suspicion that all was not well with Oxford education. "I regret to say", he said, speaking from the vantage point of his fellowship at Queen's, "that it is perfectly possible to obtain a Double First in Oxford without a sympathetic understanding of what a trade union is: and that seems to me, so far as it goes, a flaw in that system."[1]

We can now regard the W.E.A. as something more than an embryonic organism. It had a full-time secretary, a name which was becoming widely known in the educational world, a number of branches, a larger number of affiliated working-class organizations, and in 1906 it acquired an office consisting of two small rooms at 24 Buckingham Street, off the Strand. In these cramped quarters, whose rent and rates amounted to £29 3s. per annum, Mansbridge functioned as a spider in its webb. "Will you walk into my parlour said the spider to the fly?"—it is already overcrowded and we have no spare cash to pay for service rendered, but the work is there to be done; here is your job, you will surely stay and do it. . . . The Mansbridge magnetism was as magnetic as ever; volunteers came, and stayed.

But to an ever-increasing extent work was being done on the frontiers of the movement—in the branches which have been

[1] See *William Temple*, by F. A. Iremonger, p. 84.

mentioned, and in the districts which have yet to be brought into the picture. For this, provision was made in a revised constitution adopted at the 1906 Annual Meeting. Its object was defined as the promotion of "the Higher Education of Working People, primarily by the extension of University Teaching, also (a) by the assistance of working-class efforts of a specifically educational character, (b) by assistance in the development of an efficient School Continuation System, (c) by the co-ordination of popular educational effort". Its membership was to cover individuals and societies, the former paying a minimum annual subscription of one shilling, the latter of £1 1s. The executive committee was to consist of one representative from each of the following organizations: the Co-operative Union, the Association of Directors of Education, the National Home Reading Union, the Working Men's Club and Institute Union, Ruskin College, the National Union of Teachers, the Social and Political Education League and the London Working Men's College, together with eight directly elected members. The branches were to consist of two representatives from the local University Extension Centre, two from the Co-operative Society, one from each "Working-class organization of standing in the locality" and two directly elected members. The branches were to be "self-governing" but were to report at least once a quarter to the executive which might provide funds for specially approved work which the branch was unable to meet from local sources. A representative Advisory Council was to be constituted, to which matters of importance might be referred at the discretion of the executive, which was also empowered to use its discretion concerning the times and location of an annual meeting.

This constitution was clearly drafted by inexperienced constitution-makers. It has a strangely unfinished appearance. Who were to be the Association's officers? How, when, and where, was their election or appointment to be achieved—or for that matter the election of the eight executive committee members? In fact, the new constitution lasted scarcely a year. At the Annual Meeting of 1907 a new and much more representative Central Authority was brought into being in the shape of a Council consisting of representatives of the districts as well as of affiliated societies and up to ten co-opted members. The officers of the Association were also defined as consisting of a president and treasurer to be elected at an Annual General Meeting, and a secretary to be appointed by the Central Council. There was no mention of an executive committee, but since the Central Council was given power to appoint such committees as it thought necessary, it might be assumed that something in the nature of an executive committee would materialize.

The large measure of autonomy which this constitution-making assigned to branches and districts was both a cause and an effect of the diversity of local activities and the rapid multiplication of local organizations. In 1905 there were eight branches. By the summer of 1908 there were fifty. And it was in the local organizations that the real work of adult education was done. They promoted University Extension Courses and rounded up audiences for them; they poked and prodded their local education committees; they conducted propaganda for their local art galleries and museums; they formed clubs, libraries, discussion groups and reading circles; they organized educational excursions; they fastened upon local pundits and incited them to speak to the people. And everywhere and all the time they aimed at drawing into the orbit of educational endeavour, the keener spirits of their local trade-union branches and co-operative societies.

And now among the first-born of the branches there rose like a star, Rochdale, the branch whose "extreme vigour" is specially commended in the Association's Second Annual Report: Rochdale—described by Defoe in 1720 as a town "so remote, so out of the way, and so at the very foot of the moun-tains, that we may suppose it would be but little frequented". But frequented it was even then, by those who dealt in coarse textile goods, and a century later its surrounding valleys were sprouting those "dark satanic mills" which inflamed the imagi-nation of William Blake. Its remoteness made its people self-reliant and its climate made them tough. Its manufactures made them dexterous and the system under which those manufactures were operated made them conscious of certain social and economic problems for which the free-price economy of the nineteenth century offered no solution. It was in this soil that the Consumers' Co-operative Movement had struck its first tenacious roots when in 1844 the "Rochdale Pioneers" combined to run a little store of their own in Toad Lane. Even at that date co-operators were not unaware of the significance of education for those who wanted to get a decisive hand on the political and economic controls of a complex social organism. They knew that:—

You may become strong and clamorous, you may win a victory, you may effect a revolution, but you will be trodden down again under the feet of knowledge unless you get it for yourselves; even if you win that victory you will be trodden down again under the feet of knowledge if you leave knowledge in the hands of privilege, because knowledge will always win over ignorance.

Was this a rumble of thunder on the left, warning the unsuspecting workers of what *bourgeois* education had in store for them? Not at all. It was Charles Gore, Bishop of Birmingham addressing the 1909 Annual Meeting of the W.E.A. in the Wesleyan Central Hall, Sheffield. By which time Rochdale, determined that knowledge should not be left in the hands of privilege, had once again opened a chapter of working-class history and produced a new generation of "Rochdale Pioneers".

# CHAPTER FOUR

# EVOLUTION OF THE TUTORIAL CLASS

SINCE the earliest days of University Extension, the inhabitants of Rochdale had offered a ready response to the opportunities it offered. Both from the Manchester University Extension Department and from the Oxford University Extension Department, lecturers journeyed to this outpost of Lancashire industrialism and found there eager audiences. With so positive an educational tradition it is not surprising that Rochdale was one of the first areas—in fact it was the second—to form a branch of the W.E.A. This it did under the title, Rochdale Educational Guild, since the W.E.A. was not yet the W.E.A. in name, and the name that it had, did not commend itself to Rochdale. The Guild was formally constituted in March 1905, at an inaugural meeting addressed by Sydney Waterlow, newly appointed Extension Secretary to Manchester University, and Sydney Chapman, its distinguished Professor of Economics. The Guild's first year of work, as recorded in an appendix to Mansbridge's *Adventure in Working Class Education*, suggests that it had already inherited a tradition of educational vitality and local goodwill. It was indeed fortunate in having secured Hudson Shaw as one of its extension lecturers, for where he went, educational enthusiasm boiled up. Shakespeare and Ruskin, Citizenship, Economics and Homemaking, Composition and (for adults only) Arithmetic, all these were studied; also—at the request of the Carters' Union—"The Care of the Horse". Botanical specimens were collected for the local museum, excursions went forth to theatres and art galleries in Manchester—here, indeed, was an educational ferment reaching the point of effervescence. But one thing was wanting: a certainty of continuous and systematic student application; and that, in the opinion of Mansbridge, Rochdale was now ready to give. If thirty students would pledge themselves to make regular attendances and submit regular written work for a class covering two years—then, said Mansbridge, a first-rate tutor, plus financial help, would be forthcoming.

Rochdale *was* ready, provided the class was held on a Saturday afternoon to avoid the irregularities of industrial overtime. It remained for Mansbridge to fulfil his side of the bargain. In August 1907 he brought a group of prospective Rochdale students up to Oxford and presented them to the Dean of Christ Church, who was at the time chairman of the Extension Delegacy. They told the dean that if he knew how hungry they were for education he would melt down the college plate to satisfy their craving. This was not necessary. The dean gave them a good lunch and promised them a tutor. Already New College had guaranteed a special donation to the Extension Delegacy to promote precisely this kind of systematic study.

It now appeared that what Rochdale was about to have, Longton, one of the Staffordshire Five Towns, also wanted. Longton, though it had as yet no W.E.A. branch, had for some time absorbed the inspiration of Hudson Shaw, and it had E. S. Cartwright. Cartwright was a host in himself on the side of working-class education. His whole personality was aflame with enthusiasm for it and delight in it. His eyes sparkled with it; his very walk was buoyant with it. All his energies, outside the humdrum office job by which he sustained his family, were devoted to it. He had attended extension lectures and urged others to attend them. He had made contact with Mansbridge and followed the progress of the Rochdale negotiations. He was prepared to be member of a class, secretary of a class, recruiting agent of a class.

It now remained for Mansbridge and Oxford between them to produce the tutor. And here the stars in their courses fought for the W.E.A. and produced the man who was to contribute to working-class education, and indeed to the Labour Movement as a whole, that touch of intellectual distinction without which missionary zeal may easily slip across the invisible frontier which separates sentiment from sentimentality. When R. H. Tawney consented to undertake these pioneer tutorial classes he already had two valuable qualifications for the job. He was a university scholar and teacher of proved ability and he had already made a number of teaching contacts with working-class audiences and gauged their needs. Like Temple, he was an old

Rugbeian and a Balliol man. Like Temple, he had experienced the incomparable intellectual discipline of the Oxford "Greats" school. Like Temple, he had a lively natural sympathy with working-class aspirations and saw in education one means for their achievement. But though they shared political and educational ideals and were, in fact, lifelong friends, they were in many respects not in the least alike. Temple, for all his deep Christian humility, looked like what he was: a great prince of the Church. Tawney, though he spoke with the accents of Balliol and carried his head like the monarch of the glen, looked at times like a manual worker who had not bothered to tidy himself up for a collar-and-tie job. Any room inhabited by Tawney would in a short time present a scene of chaos amounting to squalor. He appeared impervious to physical discomfort and wholly devoid of worldly ambition. Unlike Temple, whose Christian charity was so unquestioning as to detract from the value of his written testimonials, Tawney had a perception of human frailty which enabled him to detect insincerity, pompousness or greed, and a mastery of English so complete that he could pierce it with a single phrase of unforgettable elegance and sting. He did not, however, encounter insincerity, pompousness or greed among his working-class students, and his carelessness of outward appearance put them at their ease. He talked to them as man to man, neither claiming authority nor asking for unquestioned agreement. But as he talked, the breadth and quality of his mind and the meticulous accuracy of his scholarship reflected itself in the work of his students and established the standard of their thought. He will probably go down to history as the greatest adult education tutor of all time as well as what he later proved himself to be, a notable explorer of England's economic history and a writer of magnificent English prose.

It was indeed fortunate that the first two tutorial classes should have been launched under Tawney's leadership, for a tradition of academic excellence was thus established for the tutors and students who came after. It was also fortunate that acceptance of physical discomfort was among Tawney's marked characteristics. In 1907 he was acting as part-time Assistant Lecturer in Economics in the University of Glasgow at a salary of £50 a year helped out by journalistic work for the *Glasgow Herald*. The salary attached to these early tutorial classes was more in the nature of token payment and the journeys involved were tedious, tiring and time-absorbing. Leaving Glasgow on a Friday morning Tawney could arrive at Longton in time for a Friday evening class. After a night at Longton he could make Rochdale in time for the 2.30 Saturday afternoon class. He would normally return to Glasgow on a Sunday, mingling with the theatrical touring companies who, with their paraphernalia of dress-baskets and stage properties, were an interesting and convivial feature of Edwardian Sunday travel. Thus was the tutorial class experiment initiated, the tutorial class model established. It was the W.E.A.'s most distinctive and significant contribution to the progress of adult education, and the finest fruit of Mansbridge's great idea of a closely integrated partnership between scholarship and labour. The next step was to build on the experience of Rochdale and Longton a tutorial class structure secure in its financial backing and national in its scope.

After somewhat protracted negotiation, the two pioneer tutorial classes started work in January 1908. But events had been moving swiftly and significantly in the background. In the summer of 1907 a conference organized by the W.E.A. at the invitation of the Oxford and Cambridge extension authorities had assembled in the Examination Schools at Oxford for the specific purpose of considering "What Oxford can do for working people". Bishop Gore presided over it. The three familiar ingredients: scholarship, co-operation and trade unionism were duly represented, and there was added a fourth ingredient of considerable significance. Sir Robert Morant and H. F. Heath represented the Board of Education.

One member of that conference, a shipwright from Portsmouth dockyard named J. M. Mactavish, was prepared to tell Oxford what it could do for working people, in words which were neither respectful nor wholly accurate, but nevertheless arresting and refreshing. "I am not here as a suppliant for my class"—thus he began. "I decline to sit at the rich man's gate praying for crumbs. I claim for my class all that Oxford has to give." He went on to explain that if Oxford was not prepared to admit that claim, so much the worse for Oxford. Indeed, in the latter part of his speech he indicated that in the matter of economics Oxford had not much to give; nothing more, in fact, than a school of economics which provides comfortable assurance for "the young gentlemen who frequent her colleges". If Oxford wants workpeople to come to Oxford, Oxford must do better than that. It must offer "a new science of national and international economics", based "not on the acquisitiveness of the individual but upon social utility". The working man does not want to escape from his class, but rather to lift his class, to return to it from Oxford inspired "not with the idea of getting on but with the idea of social service".[1] Such speeches are better heard than read. One may question the speaker's conception of the function of the economist or of the conclusions to be drawn from the teaching of economics at Oxford— though admittedly Oxford had not at that time much to boast about in regard to economic teaching and research. But Mactavish expressed himself with eloquence and force and his speech was undoubtedly the star turn of the conference if not also of his own career in the field of adult education. Without it Gore's plea for definite action might have been less effective. "What I should like to see brought about", said Gore, "is that wherever in any city there is a guaranteed class of thirty persons, or of some such number, who undertake to see to the local expenses, there I want that the universities, not Oxford and Cambridge only . . . should be willing to provide a teacher who should help the men through this systematic course of study. I believe that is what we really want."

And that is what the conference in fact accomplished. Sir Robert Morant set the seal on its accomplishment when he declared that the Board of Education was "looking for guidance from such an Association as is represented here today, to show us the way in which adult education can best be furthered. In particular we believe it is to small classes and solid, earnest work that we can give increasingly of the golden stream". This last phrase was somewhat cryptic and easily misunderstood. In those days public money seldom flowed through the

[1] For the text of Mactavish's speech see *University Tutorial Classes*, by A. Mansbridge, Appendix IX.

hands of voluntary bodies in a "golden stream". But he was indeed holding out a promise of conditional grant aid to classes of the kind foreshadowed by Gore and this was an important concession.

The conference had momentous results. Its speakers had made definite suggestions as to the kind of working-class education Oxford might provide. A resolution moved by Walter Nield of the North-Western Co-operative Education Committees' Association, and seconded by Sidney Ball of St. John's College, called for the formation of a joint committee: seven persons nominated by the Vice-Chancellor of Oxford University, and seven by the W.E.A. Executive Committee, with instructions to report to the organizations represented at the conference as to the best way of carrying out the suggestions made in the course of its deliberations. Oxford was willing. Indeed Temple asserted many years later that Mansbridge had already "squared" the Vice-Chancellor, since he was "much too knowing" to allow such a request to be made if he was not certain of its being granted. Thus, the Dean of Christ Church, chairman of the Extension Delegacy, and J. A. R. Marriott, its secretary, Professor Turner, A. L. Smith, Sidney Ball, A. E. Zimmern, and H. B. Lees-Smith, Chairman of Ruskin College, were nominated by the Vice-Chancellor, and Temple expressed a strong suspicion that they were hand-picked by Mansbridge. Meanwhile, from the W.E.A. came W. H. Berry of the Co-operative Union Education Committee, C. W. Bowerman and D. J. Shackleton, representing the Trades Union Congress, R. Campbell representing the Friendly Societies, J. M. Mactavish and Alfred Wilkinson, representing themselves as active members of the Labour Party, and Mansbridge representing the W.E.A. With Zimmern and Mansbridge acting as joint secretaries the committee set to work with the intention of producing a report by the following Easter.

Its final report did not in fact appear until the end of 1908. But even while the committee was deliberating events were moving towards fulfilment of the conference idea. As a result, the final report, when it did appear, comprised recorded experience as well as concrete suggestion, and this made it an even more valuable document than it would otherwise have been. Already Oxford University had empowered its Extension Delegacy to set up a joint committee of university and working-class representatives. Already tutorial classes on the Rochdale Longton model had started work at Chesterfield, Glossop, Littleborough, Oldham, Swindon and Wrexham. Already the influence of working-class interests had begun to make its impact on Oxford teaching. Political Science was to be included in the Economics Diploma course and the Trustees of the University Appeal Fund had urged the establishment of a lectureship in Political Theory and Institutions.

The full report, as published at the end of 1908 under the title *Oxford and Working-class Education*, constitutes a supremely important landmark in the history of adult education. This is not surprising, since it was largely the work of Tawney and Zimmern. It was more than a blue-print of an administrative plan. It was a thoughtful analysis of the history, aspirations, achievements and failures of extra-mural adult education to date, together with a searching and wholly uninhibited discussion of the part played—or not played—by Oxford University in the light of its declared objects and the intentions of its pious founders. Though much water has flowed under Folly Bridge since its publication, the report still makes interesting reading. Its recommendations concerning administrative machinery for the promotion of tutorial class work were an elaboration of what had already been evolved by the Oxford Extension Delegacy. They were set forth in sufficient detail to serve as a model for other universities and their suggested conditions for the conduct of tutorial classes presented a carefully tested scheme for the maintenance of standards sufficiently high to justify government grant-aid and to produce work of whose quality no university need be ashamed. The precise financial arrangements with their division of responsibility between the local organizing body, the universities and the public purse, were formulated with reference to the statutory grant-giving powers of local education authorities as well as of the Board of Education, and were drafted in the light of experiments already operating in various parts of the country as well as in connection with the tutorial classes already at work under the auspices of the Oxford Extension Delegacy.

By non-fictional standards the report was a "best-seller". It had an excellent press and its first edition of three thousand copies was quickly sold out. A second was forthcoming. As a result, the eight tutorial classes running under Oxford auspices by the end of 1908 had by the end of the following year grown to thirty-nine, operating under the auspices of Oxford, Cambridge, London, Manchester, Liverpool, Leeds and Sheffield Universities. All these had established joint committees on the Oxford model, and in February 1910 an unprecedented event occurred: representatives of the various universities joined forces to form a Central Joint Advisory Committee. Never before, it seems, had the universities of Great Britain achieved such an element of co-operation. According to Temple, "the Board of Education had been struggling for years to persuade the universities and university colleges to come together in any one body for any purpose that could be devised, if only they would unite on something".[1] Mansbridge succeeded where the Board had failed. The representatives of the universities were thus introduced to one another; the Vice-Chancellor of Oxford University asked a distinguished member of the gathering who he was and was informed that he was the Vice-Chancellor of the University of Manchester. The universities thus became accustomed to convene meetings for discussion of common problems and their vice-chancellors learned to recognize one another at sight. In due course a permanent Vice-Chancellors' Committee was evolved, with a secretariat, for periodic meetings. Meanwhile the Central Joint Advisory Committee which had set the ball rolling, continued to function for its own original purpose.

The tutorial class system evolved during the fateful years 1907–10 constitutes a perfect expression of the partnership between learning and labour envisaged by Mansbridge since his earliest exciting encounter with the world of scholarship. Out from the universities went the tutors: young men and women at the outset of careers in university teaching and research or professors at the peak of academic eminence;

[1] See *Highway*, November 1942, p. 9, and December 1944, p. 35.

men and women to whom the salaries meant little but to whom the work meant much because it brought them into contact with a new range of students with a new range of interests and experiences and a new intensity of response. In Tawney's first Rochdale class was a young reporter from the local paper who in due course came to write the history of the cotton industry and edit the *Manchester Guardian*. There was a young mill-hand who was destined to write the history of the W.E.A.'s early years and rule over Holybrook House. At Longton there was a young woman student who was destined to be Mayor of Stoke. In the early tutorial classes men and women of exceptional natural ability, with no more than eight years or so of board-school teaching as an educational background, were learning the art of thought and the technique of free and fair discussion as well as the discipline of systematic study. Where the extension lecturer had provided a listening audience for an inspiring lecturer, the tutorial class, based as its name indicates on the tutorial methods of the ancient universities, provided an intimate intellectual contact between teacher and student in which the give and take of discussion was an essential feature. Hence the limitation of classes to a maximum of thirty enrolled students. As time went on the results of the system were seen in the contributions made by ex-tutorial class students to W.E.A. organization; to trade-union leadership; to local government; to parliament and government office; until the time came for a former tutorial class student to preside over the educational destinies of the nation as Minister of Education.

Meanwhile, year by year, the memories of the tutors became increasingly stored with the faces and personalities of students, with discussions in schoolrooms and trade-union offices, trades and labour clubs, public libraries and village halls—discussions often prolonged beyond the point at which a disgruntled intrusive caretaker would call attention to the clock with the urgency of a conscientious publican at closing-time. There would be other memories: trains, trams, or 'buses on cross-country journeys, cars driven on ice-bound roads or piloted through almost impenetrable November fogs; summer schools, week-end schools, Saturday afternoon schools—diversified by walks over moors with the previous evening's talk still ardently continued.

So different from the single age-group fresh-from-secondary-education denizens of a university classroom! So much more diversified, so much more critical and in some respects so much more interesting!

The tutorial class movement gave as good as it got, and not only to its tutors but to scholarship in general. When the Oxford committee issued its famous report, such was the meticulous thoroughness of its authors, that they added an appendix on suggested courses of study with recommendations for reading. Contemplating the list of books in the history section, one is struck by the lamentable paucity of material relating to the economic and social aspects of the subject. How did the English peasantry come to be excluded from the land? What conditioned the revolutionary ferment of the Chartist Movement? How did the technical advances of the industrial revolution period affect the day to day lives of the workers? There was, of course, Cunningham's great pioneer economic history, there were the Webbs, there were others— but compared with the response made by generations of historians to the requirements of constitutionalists, dynasts and military tacticians there was precious little. Yet these were the very kind of questions which most vitally concerned working-class students. They wanted to know something of the forces which had made them what they were. They wanted to gauge the possibility of controlling and directing those forces, so that they might become what they wanted to be.

During the four decades which followed the inception of the tutorial class movement, scholars of the calibre of Tawney, Cole, J. L. and Barbara Hammond—to mention only a few— have provided material which may help us to frame answers to such questions. A new direction and a new stimulus has been given to historical research. *Post hoc ergo propter hoc* is a dangerous form of argument, and various causes including the insatiable and sometimes seemingly pointless curiosity of scholars have contributed to this latter-day emphasis on the social and economic aspects of history. After all, Sidney and Beatrice Webb were already well away with their study of trade-union and co-operative history and they had little contact with the W.E.A. and sought their inspiration elsewhere. But

William Temple, preaching during the last year of his life in the University Church of Oxford, chose to associate this particular phase of scholarship with the demands of working-class higher education; and scholarship was, he said, the richer for it. It is not for an obscure historian of the W.E.A. to question the considered verdict of a learned archbishop—though it is possible that the archbishop was in this connection not wholly unbiased.

# CHAPTER FIVE

# THE W.E.A. GROWS UP

ALL good causes require for healthy growth a stimulating breath of opposition, and every experienced class tutor is aware of how much he owes to the Marxist member of the history or economics class who can be counted on to provide this valuable ingredient. One may be tempted to speculate on the part which the Church might yet play in the nation's consciousness if sermons were followed by open discussion and if a few convinced atheists could be persuaded to attend divine service. In this respect the W.E.A. was not richly served. It almost seemed as though from the very start all men spoke well of it and praised it—a state of affairs for whose dangers we have scriptural authority. But not quite all. From its earliest days there had been a rumble of thunder on the left, and when the W.E.A. had appeared to make headway in trade-union circles, Mansbridge was able to record the existence of active opposition. It came, to begin with, from the activities of a certain Mrs. Bridges Adams, who professed a particular concern for trade-union education. Mrs. Adams had a profound distrust of universities. They were in her opinion citadels of class-privilege whose denizens were dedicated to its preservation. If they were prepared to patronize the efforts of Mansbridge and his friends, it could only be because they hoped to divert him from uncontrolled activities which might otherwise subvert the privileged position of the rich, and to inoculate him with economic doctrines likely to render him tolerant, if not appreciative of the *status quo*. Not through such contacts lay the road to working-class emancipation. So active was Mrs. Bridges Adams in support of this contention that Mansbridge notes in his autobiography[1] that during his Association's early years "it became impossible to hold an advertised meeting anywhere without her intrusion, or that of her commissioned friends". Indeed, he refers to an assertion on her part that she was in possession of documentary evidence

[1] See *The Trodden Road*, by A. Mansbridge, p. 63.

to prove that he was paid by the universities to side-track the
working classes from any participation in university benefits.
She might very easily have obtained documentary proof that
he was "paid by the universities" since part of his meagre
salary as General Secretary was contributed by university
supporters, and W.E.A. finances were not conducted in secret.
But concerning the purpose of such payment she was strangely
misinformed. Nevertheless, her suspicions and those of her trade-
union friends were not altogether unnatural. Persons who enjoy
a privileged position do not readily abandon it. In the business
world, or the world of collective bargaining with which trade-
unions are concerned, it would be safe to say that those who
enjoy a privileged position never readily abandon it—they have
to be forced out of it. And, moreover, it must be remembered
that the early activities of the W.E.A. were carried on within
the framework of the class structure described in Chapter One.
Group antagonisms were well defined and acute—as were the
differences of dress, speech and habit which reflected them.
It is not surprising that among the early opponents of
Mansbridge's plan for working-class education we find some
notable names; those of John Scurr, for instance, and in very
early days, George Lansbury.

In 1907 a new phase opened in the development of an
articulate opposition. It was precipitated by events at Ruskin
College, Oxford, which in that year appealed for financial
support from the trade-union movement. It happened also to
be the year of that historic Oxford conference which led to the
publication of the report on *Oxford and Working-class Education*,
and to the initiation of the tutorial class system. The first event
raised the question whether a non-partisan college largely controlled by university men could in fact supply the kind of
economic teaching required as a theoretical basis for a militant
Labour Movement. The second appeared to commit working-
class aspirations to a school of economics devised by middle-class
economists as an apology for the existing capitalist system. To
those plagued by such doubts, the Marxist doctrine of surplus
value and the law of capitalist accumulation seemed emo-
tionally satisfying by reason of its authoritative presentation and
its association of commodity values with honest human sweat.

It was at the same time intellectually satisfying by reason of its intricate argument and its appearance of mathematical precision. There is no doubt that Marx's *Das Kapital* was, and still is, an exceedingly impressive book—especially to those who are not able fully to understand it, or having understood it, are not able to relate it to its historical background. At any rate this was the kind of teaching demanded by an ardent group of Ruskin College students.

But while prepared to recognize, as Gore and Temple had recognized, the limitations of Oxford scholarship in relation to the interests and experiences of working-class students, the leaders of the W.E.A. were not prepared to compromise on what they regarded as an objective search for truth. Nor would they admit that an objective analysis on orthodox lines of the working of a free-price economy necessarily constitutes an *apologia* for that system—or rather lack of system. Certainly John Stuart Mill had not so regarded it in 1848. Thus between the study of *what* to think and the study of *how* to think, a great gulf seemed to yawn, and the W.E.A. was irrevocably committed to the latter process. Meanwhile a strike of Ruskin students against what they regarded as tendentious *bourgeois* teaching led to a mass secession from their college and ultimately to the establishment of a rival adult education body, the Labour Colleges supported by the Plebs League which in due course evolved into the National Council of Labour Colleges, a body destined to play an active part in a later phase of W.E.A. history. Its proud boast from the first was that it received no financial assistance from state or capitalist sources and that its teaching was—and is—thus unconstrained by any obligation to serve the interests of those in power.

It may be added that the strike of Ruskin students led the governing body of that College to look to its own composition, with the result that in 1909 the representation on it of working-class organizations was greatly strengthened.

This emergence of an organized opposition at the moment when the W.E.A. was giving practical shape to its concordat with the universities emphasizes the significance of Mactavish's spectacular utterance at the historic Oxford conference of 1907. The force and fury of his condemnation of Oxford economics could scarcely be improved on by the most bitterly disgruntled Ruskin secessionist. But it had led Mactavish, and those who listened to him, to the conclusion that Oxford might be licked into shape—or in other words, achieve salvation by working-class influence. Thus the suspicions of a potential opposition were harnessed to the constructive task of peaceful penetration, with results which Temple was able to record in his university sermon preached many years later.

To judge from the statistical records of W.E.A. progress during these years, criticism of its policy offered little impediment either to the growth of its membership, the multiplication of its branches, the popularity of its tutorial classes, or the increase of its affiliated working-class and other organizations. In 1907 it recorded 4,343 individual members, 47 branches, and 622 affiliated bodies of which 252 were trade unions or trade-union branches. These figures grew steadily year by year and their growth demanded an increasingly powerful and complex organization. At the centre in London, the business of directing so expansive a body soon outgrew the two small rooms in Adam Street, Adelphi, and in 1911 a move was made to 14 Red Lion Square, off Holborn, an equally good central position boasting three first-floor rooms; a small room for the general secretary, and a larger outer and inner office for all the rest, including the storage, sorting and packing of literature. It was, of course, not long before the new office was as uncomfortably congested as the old had been.

The perpetual headache at headquarters was, as it usually is with an expanding and exuberant organization, finance. There was never enough of it. In its second year the Association's income reached three figures and its expenditure remained well in hand. In 1906 the appeal for £500 a year guaranteed for five years to support an office and full-time secretary, produced £108 guaranteed for two years. In 1907 it nearly reached the £500 figure and the general fund was still solvent. But in 1908 the W.E.A. was "in the red" with an income of £267 to cover expenditure of £272.

This was the year in which the Central Office promoted what was perhaps the most spectacular University Extension Course ever held. It consisted of a course of Saturday afternoon lectures on *The House of Commons*, given by Canon J. H. B. Masterman in the Royal Gallery of the House of Lords, by permission of the Lord Chamberlain and the First Commissioner of Works, under suasion from J. Ramsay MacDonald, M.P. Admission was free and demand for admission intense; but only one thousand could be accommodated and tickets were distributed through affiliated organizations. Week by week there appeared in Palace Yard a phenomenon which, had our forebears but known it, foreshadowed the cinema queues of a later civilization.

This was also the year in which the W.E.A. matured plans for the publication of its own monthly journal: the *Highway*, so called as an indication of its promoter's hope that by such a route, rather than from rung to rung of a narrow "educational ladder", would the workers of Great Britain march, no longer in single file, to the goal of higher education. It was a distant hope, for even the "educational ladder" as it existed in 1907 seemed rather to merit the name conferred upon it by R. H. Tawney, of an educational "greasy pole", since so many climbers fell off before reaching the top.

On October 1st, 1908, the first issue of the *Highway* appeared, and from the beginning its editor was able to draw upon a wide range of first-class literary talent. Margaret Macmillan, A. D. Lindsay, Arthur Greenwood, A. E. Zimmern, Maude Royden, were frequent contributors. But it is invidious to select names for so many gave their services and gave of their best.

It is small wonder that during these years the W.E.A. frequently found itself "in the red". This did not appear seriously to cramp its style. In 1909 it launched out in a new direction. In the majority of classes it was noted that males constituted the overwhelming majority. Where were the women? It was a natural deduction that most of them were at home, "sitting in" while their husbands, brothers, fathers, as the case might be, pursued the higher learning elsewhere. And as politically minded beings the women were certainly backward. It was nobody's business to see that they were not; for in these far-off days with which we are concerned it must be remembered that they had no votes. Political propagandists were not interested in them. The founder and proprietor of the *Daily Mail*, however, was. He had in fact provided for their special delectation the *Daily Mirror*—an illustrated daily, catering for the supposed taste of the sex which, as he put it, "can't write and doesn't want to read". Women were ever the victims of rash and sweeping generalizations, and statements about their backwardness may be both rash and sweeping. But the educational process was not made easy for them either by their domestic circumstances or the attention paid to their needs.

The W.E.A. was not content to leave it at that. And incidentally, from the point of view of the men it would have been bad policy. Few things are more discouraging to an intellectually enterprising husband than the companionship of a wife who is unable either to share or understand the intellectual activities which take him out of an evening.

So having launched the *Highway*, the Central Office began to devote serious attention to the women. In 1909 a Women's Advisory Committee was established. Mrs. Mansbridge was, of course, an active member of it; so was Julia Madams of the Co-operative Union. It was clear to the committee that a large number of women, if they were to be drawn into the educational sphere of influence, must have special classes at special hours suited to their pattern of working life. The early afternoon was indicated, when the older children were at school and the husbands still at work. Indeed, from many points of view women presented a special problem of organization—so much so that a year later a full-time organizer was appointed for work on their behalf. To realize the thought and energy that was put into this business one has only to read the articles which month by month Maude Royden contributed to the *Highway*. She was campaigning on behalf of working-women's education with the zest which a little later she devoted to the cause of Women's Suffrage. It was, of course, the same cause.

But all this cost more and still more money. Income increased because expanding activities brought a measure of expanding financial support. But the activities increased faster than the financial support. The "golden stream" from the Board of Education, swollen in varying degrees by little silver streams from local education authorities, sustained the full-fledged tutorial classes. But the very generosity of local authorities to the tutorial classes meant a diversion of potential assistance from the W.E.A.'s wider activities.

In 1911 a *cri du cœur* went up from the Central Office. If only the affiliated societies would give more than the bare guinea required by the constitution! There can be no doubt that the tutorial classes were making very heavy demands both on the finances and the organizing potential of the Association—for except in the case of those operating under London University, the work of organizing the tutorial classes fell upon the officers of the W.E.A.

Nevertheless, the tutorial classes were the brightest jewels in the W.E.A. crown, and money and labour spent on them were well spent. They were the standard-bearers of W.E.A. education. They upheld its quality and preserved the intellectual life-giving link with university scholarship. Where they flourished, branch organization also flourished. As the Annual Report for 1910 notes, "where a branch has a tutorial class it develops a strong educational backbone". And it was the work of the tutorial classes that consolidated the prestige of the W.E.A. in official as well as academic circles—especially after the publication of a report on their work by Professor Hobhouse and J. W. Headlam, H.M.I., made at the instance of the Board of Education in 1911.

This report was based on visits of inspection to fourteen classes, including access to the actual written work of the students and talks with them and their tutors. Among the tutors inspected was R. H. Tawney, Professor Ramsay Muir, R. V. Lennard, Gilbert Slater and Walter Layton. The subsequent report was not uncritical nor was there any attempt to minimize the difficulty of handling students with a wide variety of educational background, with an insufficiency of leisure for reading and essay work, and often with inadequate opportunities for peace and quiet at home. The report was, however, imaginative and appreciative as well as informative to those unacquainted with the procedure and purpose of the tutorial class—and its conclusion was unequivocal. "Of the quality of training and its potentialities of social value" the authors had formed "a high estimate". They "had no hesitation in saying that the money contributed by the Board for the support of these classes is being put to a thoroughly good use. They are establishing in a number of great industrial towns, centres of genuinely educational thought on social and industrial problems. What they teach is no mere exotic of culture, but is intimately related to the life and work of the students. Its effects are, therefore, likely to be permanent, and to spread from the actual members of the class to those who come in contact with them. If it comes to be the custom for those who take an interest in public affairs to prepare themselves by attending courses of this kind, the results may be of considerable importance. At any rate, much will have been done to diffuse among large classes of the population, to whom it has until lately been wholly unfamiliar, a new idea of the possibilities of education on these matters".[1] Thus the report concludes.

Already the effects of tutorial classes were beginning "to spread from the actual members of the class to those who come in contact with them". From the Longton class, led by E. S. Cartwright, members went forth to the miners of North Staffs: and educational work sprouted in six villages. Round Swindon something in the nature of a rural educational revival was noted. And into the W.E.A. Central Office, with its district and branch organizations, tutorial class members were "ploughing back" as tutors and organizers the education they had acquired as members of tutorial classes. But to understand the full significance of this process it is necessary to bring into the picture an element of W.E.A. organization hitherto ignored, not because it is unimportant, but because it is so important as to merit particular treatment: the districts and the district secretaries.

[1] The text of this report appears as Appendix III to Mansbridge's *University Tutorial Classes*.

As early as 1905 we can note developments which foreshadow the evolution of the W.E.A. districts. The Annual Report for that year records the appointment of Y. Pickles of Blackley as honorary secretary of a North-Western area committee as the result of a conference held in the Whitworth Hall of Manchester University, also of J. White of Torquay for the South-West, as the result of a similar conference at Exeter. In the following year W. J. Sharkey of Birmingham appears as honorary secretary of a Midland area committee, and there is mention of a "provisional committee" for South Wales and Monmouthshire. Meanwhile at Birmingham activities were under way to secure a guaranteed income for the appointment of a full-time secretary for the Midlands.

A year later we learn that the North-Western committee had divided its territory between the North-West and the North-East, and yet another year later, that an appeal was out for a full-time secretary for the North-West.

By 1908 organization by districts had taken shape. Three districts had achieved full-time secretaries: the Midlands with J. Sharkey (soon to be succeeded by T. W. Price, an old Rochdalian), the North-Western District with L. V. Gill (another old Rochdalian) and South Wales with A. C. Willis. The South-Western district organization was in temporary abeyance owing to the death of its honorary secretary, but it revived a year later with W. H. Watkins as secretary, and with a newly formed Southern District on its frontier, under H. E. Curtis. By which time we note that twenty-seven branches had attached themselves to their respective districts, leaving twenty-three attached to the Central Office. This was a significant advance towards the decentralization involving local autonomy which had always been a guiding principle of W.E.A. organization. It may be remembered that in 1907 a revised constitution was adopted which brought the district organizations into the picture by the representation of the districts as such, on the Central Council which governed the W.E.A.

In the years which followed, we can observe a steady expansion and elaboration of the district pattern of organization. New districts were carved out of old; there were changes in the district secretaryships, some redrafting of frontiers, and some coming-and-going as between appointments to the district and central offices. A North-Eastern District centred on Newcastle was consolidated in 1909; a London District with H. Goodman as secretary appears in 1912; and in 1913 G. H. Thompson set to work to organize a Yorkshire District, comprising the massive industrial area of the West Riding. He became its district secretary a year later, and in that office he continued with a short break until his retirement in 1945 as a leading personality of the adult education world, whose driving energy and expanding wisdom had done much to make the Yorkshire area a stronghold of educational progress and distinguished labour representation in public life.

Many years later, looking back on nearly half a century of W.E.A. activity, in the course of a parting tribute to another great district secretary, R. H. Tawney described the district office as the "strategic position" of the W.E.A. Upon the district secretary who administered that office devolved a complex of tasks which made the job no "bed of roses". He had to negotitate with the universities, administer intricate Board of Education regulations, bargain with local authorities, and conduct a steady propaganda campaign among trade-union branches. He had to do much else, and to that much else was added the multiform problems generated by insufficient cash and inadequate staff. The job of district secretary was—and is—a harassing one, and by comparable academic and civil service standards a job which is ill-remunerated in respect of the qualities and experience required for its performance. But it is a job which yields perceptible results, though these cannot be adequately expressed in facts and figures. One can record with precision the branch membership, the tutorial class attendance, the income and expenditure of a district; but one cannot record with any precision the growth of intellectual vitality, public service consciousness, or educational activity of the district in question, nor can one determine with accuracy what measure of responsibility for such growth should be assigned to the W.E.A. district organization. An industrious social researcher, prepared to analyse the personnel and proceedings of a large number of local education committees from 1903 onwards, might throw some clear light on the contribution made by W.E.A. men and women in this particular sphere of life—but it would be a big job.

Two more significant developments remain to be recorded before the story of the W.E.A.'s first decade is brought to a close by an event which will serve as a convenient chapter-ending for its history, as well as for the history of the entire civilized world.

The first is the growth of a library service to meet the very real difficulty noted by Hobhouse and Headlam in their report to the Board of Education, and all too familiar to the students and tutors of the early tutorial classes. It is clear, thus runs the report, "that the amount of reading is to a considerable extent limited by the difficulties in the supply of books. It is usual for the university to which the course is attached to send to the centre a box of books; Manchester assigns £5 for this purpose to each centre; Oxford and Cambridge send a good supply. In addition to this there are available at some centres those books which are in the Public Library. This source of supply is, however, very uncertain . . .". It is far less uncertain today; and in addition to the expansion of the public library service, *Penguin Books* now makes available a wealth of material on history, economics, philosophy, literature, science and art, at prices which, though they increase with paper and printing costs, still compare favourably with the cost of a packet of cigarettes or a seat at the cinema. Things were not so good in 1909; and the authors of the Board of Education report spoke nothing but the truth when they asserted that "the whole question of books is one that requires most urgent attention".

The Central Office did not need to be told that. For some time before 1912 the possibility of building up a central library, available for W.E.A. students all over the country, had been discussed. In 1912, thanks to the collaboration of Toynbee Hall, a start was made. Toynbee Hall provided the accommoda-tion and a nucleus of books. A joint committee of Toynbee Hall and the W.E.A. took responsibility for the library, and from the word "go" the demands on it justified its existence. But it was not enough. The library needed not merely a wider range of books, but for obvious reasons, multiplication of the same book. For instance, if a dozen classes of twenty-five members each were studying modern social history, how many copies of Hammond's *Village Labourer* would be simultaneously demanded? And if more books were needed, so too was more space to put them in and more people to handle them.

Wherever support was needed for library expansion, the Carnegie United Kingdom Trust offered possibilities, and to its trustees Mansbridge now turned. They were not unresponsive. If an "established body" would make an application, the trustees would be prepared to contribute £600 toward the establishment of a central library for students; £200 for the purchase of books and £400 a year for maintenance—on condition that an annual income of at least £320 from private subscriptions was guaranteed. Mansbridge was prepared to fulfil both conditions. He found a guarantor, and for an "established body" he produced the Central Joint Advisory Committee, weighty with university representation. In 1916 the National Central Library was established at 20 Tavistock Square, Bloomsbury—a habitation which it very quickly outgrew. It was now an independent entity, bound to the service of all students, not only those of the W.E.A. But Mansbridge, whose tactful midwifery had brought it to birth, became its chairman.

The second development was the initiation of the W.E.A. summer schools, which became and remained one of the happiest items in the store-house of W.E.A. memories. A number of W.E.A. students had from very early days been in the habit of attending the annual University Extension Summer Meetings in either Oxford or Cambridge. Indeed, it was under the auspices of such a meeting that the Association had been transformed from a provisional committee into a permanent organization. But in 1910 a summer school for tutorial class members was organized by the Oxford Tutorial Classes Committee in Oxford. It lasted eight weeks, during July and August, and eighty-nine students attended for periods of either a week or a fortnight. They paid their own costs with the assistance of grants from the Oxford Tutorial Classes Committee and the W.E.A., and a group of women students was financed through a fund contributed by women university dons. Tuition was given free by those members of Oxford University who were interested in working-class education.

Among those who were not, were one or two who wondered what Oxford was coming to when in the following year male W.E.A. students were given rooms in Balliol College whose precincts were thus not so silent as some people had hoped they might be in the welcome absence of undergraduates. In due course the example of Oxford was followed by Cambridge, London and Durham, and by Manchester in co-operation with Liverpool and the University College of North Wales. But the Oxford summer school remained for many years the longest and the largest.

Summer days in Oxford must stick in the memories of many W.E.A. students, old and young, today: mornings in college lecture rooms or sitting round the table in a tutor's book-lined study—afternoons on the river—talk, talk, talk, flowing along the tow-path of the Isis, through the glades of Bagley Wood, up and down "the High"—and in the evenings, more talk perhaps in organized discussion ("Does the Press mould public opinion or does public opinion mould the Press?")—or in lighter moods, singing: "Solomon Levi", "On Ilkla' Moor 'baht 'at" sung as men from Yorkshire know how to make men from elsewhere sing it—until it is time, and high time, for the women students to adjourn to their lodgings in St. John Street, to the gentle strains of "Good-night Ladies" issuing from the open windows overlooking a college garden. But quite a lot of work was done in these summer schools because their members were in many cases for the first time in their lives since board-school days, full-time students; and full-time students have quite a lot of time in which to play.

So ends the first decade of W.E.A. history. It will be helpful to stand for a moment with our backs to the curtain which hides the future, and take stock of what the opening months of 1914 have to show.

We see an Association of preponderantly working-class students, men and women but far more men than women, which has, to quote a phrase used by Ernest Green, been successfully "universitized" thanks to the genius of Mansbridge.[1] The trade-union movement is interested, indeed co-operative and responsive; but to quote Ernest Green again, has so far

[1] See *Highway*, October 1950.

shown little evidence of educational initiative. The Association has, however, 2,555 affiliated organizations of which 953 are trade unions, trades councils, or trade-union branches. And the Parliamentary Committee of the Trades Union Congress has just decided to affiliate to the central organization of the W.E.A. and has nominated its chairman, J. A. Seddon, as T.U.C. representative on the W.E.A. Central Council.

In addition to its affiliated bodies the Association has 179 branches and 11,430 individual members. There should be more—but unfortunately those who join classes have an obstinate bad habit of assuming that membership of a class makes them members of the W.E.A. and that this is enough. It is not, of course, and never will be. Much more is required of them than class attendance. They must be missionaries of education, giving as well as getting. When will they learn?

In the tutorial classes there are 3,343 students working under Board of Education regulations as to attendance and essay-writing in 145 classes operating under fourteen university joint committees with a Central Joint Advisory Committee to keep them in step with one another. There are any number of less exacting courses of study designed for the weaker brethren and aimed at preparing them for work of tutorial class standard. In addition to the financial backing given to the tutorial classes by the Board of Education and the universities, 57 local education authorities are giving grants for W.E.A. work, from London's contribution of £600 for up to fifteen tutorial classes, to Swansea's guinea to assist work in the Welsh area. The most usual local contribution appears to be £10 or £15 towards the expense of one tutorial class.

Finances are precarious and district autonomy renders them even more so. Autonomy does not necessarily involve financial self-support and the Central Association is burdened with the necessity of paying out £359 0s. 1d. in grants to districts out of an income which is calculated as £1,300 short of needs. Clearly this state of affairs cannot go on, and the Central Council has a drastic plan of financial reform up its sleeve for presentation to the forthcoming Annual General Meeting. It involves a high degree of centralization and a substantial increase of subscriptions and affiliation fees.

The governing body of the Association is still the Central Council with seventy-five members, ten of them elected by ballot, and the rest representative of districts and affiliated societies. The executive committee "appointed by the Council from its body and subject to it" implements the Council's decisions. Mansbridge's old friend and fellow prophet, Margaret Macmillan, is a member of it. But it is perhaps invidious to select one name. The whole Council is rich in names of men and women eminent, or in process of becoming so, in academic and labour circles. The W.E.A. can clearly command a high degree of public confidence. Its opinion must, surely, count on educational matters. In fact it does.

At the Central Office in Red Lion Square, Mansbridge has returned to his General Secretary's desk in March after a seventeen weeks' tour in Australia, New Zealand and Canada with Mrs. Mansbridge. He started it as a tired man, but that did not induce him to make a holiday of it. He swept through two continents on a tide of persuasive oratory, leaving a trail of sprouting Dominion W.E.A.s in his wake. At home, he is now regarded as an elder statesman of the educational world with innumerable interests and responsibilities outside Red Lion Square, and the secretarial work of the W.E.A. But the staff at Red Lion Square is now a little more adequate to its needs. Mansbridge's indefatigable private secretary, Miss Dorothy Jones, now functions as assistant secretary to the Association; E. W. Wimble, has been appointed financial secretary, and Miss Ida Hony administers a women's department. The women are coming on well and there is a particularly encouraging response from them in the rural areas in which there is as yet no competition from radio, television, Women's Institutes or bus services to easily accessible cinemas.

Nine districts are at work with full-time secretaries: Eastern, London, Midland, North-East, North-West, South-East (served by E. W. Wimble, in combination with his financial duties at Red Lion Square), Wales, Western, and Yorkshire the latest born. Again, it seems invidious to select names, yet it is inter-. esting to note that Will Crooks, M.P., has become chairman of the London District, Sir Oliver Lodge of the Midland, and Arthur Greenwood, with a great career still ahead of him, of the

Yorkshire District. And the chairman of the Western District is the Grand Old Man of Swindon, Reuben George.

The *Highway* is going strong with a circulation of 10,000 which falls off somewhat when classes close down for the summer, and the Toynbee Hall central library having completed two years of work, is turning over close on a thousand books and crying out for more. All would appear to be set fair for five summer schools projected for July and August, 1914, Oxford leading with an eight weeks' school to accommodate close on 150 students, London and Cambridge lagging behind somewhat with twenty-two students for a fortnight.

But all was not set fair. On June 10th, Mansbridge attended a meeting of the Selborne Committee on Church and State. He rose to speak, began—and fell back insensible. He was taken to Westminster Hospital and Mrs. Mansbridge was hastily summoned from the business of moving into a new flat. What was the matter with him? Nobody knew. Was he, perhaps, a drug-addict? Certainly not. He was not any kind of an addict unless perhaps a work-addict, but that would not account for his state of insensibility. One thing was obvious: he was very ill indeed. It was doubtful whether he would survive—and if he did, in what sort of mental or physical state would he survive? So after a few days of continued unenlightenment he was handed back to Mrs. Mansbridge, who put him to bed in the new flat, and summoned an old friend—who had many years earlier been an old enemy of left-wing persuasion—Doctor Gye of the Imperial Cancer Research Fund Laboratory. Doctor Gye thought it looked like cerebro-spinal meningitis and called in Sir Henry Head of the London Hospital, who confirmed his opinion. Thanks to accurate diagnosis, Mrs. Mansbridge's inspired amateur nursing, a long period of convalescence in the peace and quiet of Bishop Gore's house at Cuddesdon, and his own will to live, Mansbridge recovered—slowly and in the end by some miracle, completely.

Of the second and far greater event which shattered the hopeful forecasts of New Year 1914, Mansbridge was at the time scarcely conscious. On August 4th England went to war with Germany, and how that was going to affect educational advance was anybody's guess.

# CHAPTER SIX

# WORLD WAR NUMBER ONE

On August 4th, 1914, war broke over the people of Great Britain bound for their summer holidays, over an unsuspecting W.E.A. summer school lapped in the higher learning of Oxford University, over the insensible head of Mansbridge on his slow return to life, and over T. W. Price and Dorothy Jones grappling, in his absence, with the expanding work of the Central Office.

What was to be the response of the W.E.A. to this bloodshot dawn over an unfamiliar and terrifying landscape? There were some who believed that all would be over by Christmas. The German Emperor was among their number. Others, such as Lord Kitchener, darkly prophesied three years of gruelling hostility. "What will be the population of London or Manchester, or Chemnitz or Bremen, or Milan", at the end of a European war—say, between the Triple Alliance and the Triple Entente? This question had been asked by Graham Wallas early in 1914 in his formidable analysis of the world's precarious cash nexus: *The Great Society*. Nobody knew the answer. Faced with this prodigious question-mark it seemed almost frivolous to be thinking of next year's tutorial class programme or even the gradual evolution of an educated democracy. There might not be a next year, and democracy was about to fight for its life with such education as it had.

The great organization which stood for women's emancipation did not hesitate. Its organizing potential was switched from feminist propaganda to war work: hospitals, munition making, civilian relief as the case might be. Such response was not uncommon among propagandist bodies—the W.E.A. might logically have taken that line. But it did not. Its only major concession to the urgency of the moment was to cancel its Annual General Meeting planned for the autumn of 1914 and to call for increased activity in the districts as an alternative. In announcing this postponement to the Association,

Temple wrote: "Every district has been asked to hold a district meeting; and if dates permit I hope to be present at all or most of them, to urge again what I now say: this crisis proves the need for our work as it has never been proved before; let us then be up and doing". In a presidential message to the October *Highway* he spoke with even greater urgency. "England needs and still more will need the influence of a fully informed democracy if the wisest and justest end of this conflict is to be reached. I am not at all urging that classes studying other subjects should change in the middle of their course, unless intensely eager to do so. But I do urge that all who never thought or studied before should think and study now. It is not for us to assume conclusions and then look for evidence by which we can support them. Our task is to seek the truth so far as we can find it."

This, then, was the W.E.A.'s response to a war situation. It was to "keep its powder dry" and train its guns on a new menace presented by an old enemy: sloppy thought at the mercy of emotional urges: sloppy thought about the nature of the world's crisis and the forces which had brought civilized humanity to this ugly pass. By the beginning of 1915, 45 tutorial classes and 154 one-year courses and study circles were at work on subjects bearing on the war situation, and lectures were being organized up and down the country and in military camps.

Meanwhile, the *Highway* played its part, appearing month by month with articles on the politics and economics of one or another of the belligerent States.

In this war effort the reputation of the W.E.A. for objective discussion stood it in good stead. Its tutors and lecturers were handling controversial material in an environment highly charged with emotion and irrational responses to disturbing events. Charges of pacifism or pro-Germanism came very readily to certain sections of the Press, and some leading W.E.A. personalities were, indeed, peace propagandists or conscientious objectors to military service. But as the Annual Report for this difficult first year of war records: "Lecturers and students have come quite freely to the rooms and none have been asked 'what is your position?' when once it was clear that they were competent to lecture or anxious to learn. Newspaper reports have at times created difficulties, but no one has sought to use our platform for ulterior motives and the question of avoiding any specific lecturer has never seriously arisen." In November 1917, when occurrences in Russia had directed attention to the practical possibilities of violent revolution in the modern world, "a certain Professor Arnold", to quote an entry in Beatrice Webb's diary[1] "sent in the most alarmist memorandum to some members of the Cabinet—a document which was solemnly discussed. Not only the Central Labour College was denounced, but also the Workers' Educational Association cited as spreading revolutionary ideas in the guise of university education for the working class. The secretary of the W.E.A.— Mactavish—was called upon to answer this accusation—and both the accusation and the defence were despatched to Buckingham Palace". She adds that a royal summons was then issued to Mactavish. From other sources we learn that a personal encounter took place between Mactavish and King George V and that as a result of Mactavish's convincing persuasiveness His Majesty offered to become a subscriber to the W.E.A. The executive, in the discretion of its wisdom, refused to accept the royal recruit—whose adherence would have given pleasure to the Central Labour College as an example of the W.E.A.'s dubious contacts. But since its rejection would, doubtless, have given pain in other quarters—since George V was a well-loved monarch—the offer was not given publicity.

Yet, absurd as this kind of witch-hunt may appear, it could be argued that Professor Arnold was not far wrong in suspecting the spread of revolutionary ideas by the W.E.A. It all depends on what one means by "revolutionary". Nobody in the W.E.A. would have lifted up a finger to shoot a capitalist exploiter, or raise a street barricade against the defenders of class privilege. Nobody in the W.E.A. would have lifted up his voice to incite others to such activity or even to admit its social usefulness. But a re-examination of the class-structure outlined in Chapter One, may very well lead to the conclusion that the complete equality of educational opportunity which the W.E.A. was at

[1] *Beatrice Webb's Diaries 1912-24*, edited by Margaret I. Cole, p. 97.

that time vociferously advocating under the presidency of an ex-public-school headmaster, later to become an archbishop, was as subversive a revolutionary measure in its long-run effects, as any reasonable revolutionary could desire.

If it managed to escape controversial entanglements, the years 1914 and 1915 brought difficulties of another kind. During the first six months of the war the W.E.A. was without its General Secretary—though this was compensated by the unstinted devotion and quiet efficiency of T. W. Price and Dorothy Jones. Both had watched the W.E.A. grow from early days and helped it to grow. Both were wholly familiar with its ways, its personalities, its ideals, its outside contacts. By the middle of September 1914, Mansbridge was able to put pen to paper in a message of greeting to his beloved W.E.A. He hoped, he said, to be back by the beginning of 1915—and back he surely came, to shoulder burdens greater than he was now able to bear. Meanwhile Lowth, who had functioned at head-quarters as organizer for trade unions, volunteered for active service and marched away. So did A. L. Dakyns, secretary for overseas work, and W. Hosford, who ran the book department, and Wimble the finance officer. Work at the Central Office became difficult.

It was scarcely easier outside. Tawney, determined to fight by the side of those among whom he delighted to work, en-listed in the Twenty-Second Manchesters, forswearing a com-mission. Up and down the country classes lost their tutors, and tutors lost their students. Branches lost their honorary officers and membership was depleted by the call to arms or by absorption in war-work at home. Two hundred tutorial classes were due to start work in the autumn of 1914; 152 actually met. But many of these shrank below Board of Education require-ments by the end of the session and it was fortunate for W.E.A. finances that the Board took a sympathetic view of the situation and tempered the financial wind to the shorn class-register. World War Number One taught the organizers of World War Number Two that for an all-out national effort, careful direction and conservation of man-power is necessary from the word "go". There was no such direction and conservation in 1914. Volunteers for the fighting forces were called for, and volunteers came—from essential war industries, from scientific research, from teaching and administration—and month by month the casualty lists grew and month by month the personal losses of the W.E.A. were recorded in the *Highway*.

The *Highway*, too, had its difficulties under the pinch of reduced circulation and mounting costs. It grew visibly thinner as the war years rolled by. Its district supplements were dropped and plans for getting it on to the open market were put into cold storage. Starting with twenty-eight pages in 1914 it had become a mere ten-page wraith by the end of the war. But in quality it made up for what it lacked in quantity. Its earlier war job of educating its readers on the complexities of the European situation gradually gave place to its later job of providing material for a great national campaign of educational advance on the home front. And at no time does it appear to have suffered any diminution of its power to command the services of first-class contributors. G. D. H. Cole, who had emerged from Magdalen College, Oxford, as a significant and, indeed, disturbing figure in the Socialist movement during the years immediately preceding the war, became its most constant contributor on labour questions. Sanderson Furniss, a former tutor of Ruskin College, who later became its Principal, expounded economics in its columns. And the *Highway*'s circulation never ceased to be of value to the Association as a medium for conveying news of adult education activities during a period when movement to and from meetings and conferences became increasingly difficult—though as the Annual Report for 1915 points out, "it has not so far succeeded in giving all-round satisfaction". Of course it had not: it never will: never could. It has to satisfy too many different people interested in too many different subjects at too many different levels of educational experience. And it has to steer a middle way between those who want a magazine of information about W.E.A. doings and those who want a cheap substitute for the *New Statesman* or the *Spectator*; and there *is* no middle way—merely a succession of lurches from side to side.

Under war conditions the W.E.A. soon found that educational work was not enough. It had always offered its members something more than education. It had offered them intellectual companionship: the *social* pursuit of education. One expression of this bond had been the W.E.A. Comradeship Fund which Mrs. Mansbridge had organized and administered for helping W.E.A. members in difficulty. At the outset of war this little piece of organization held out a hand to members on active service and to their relatives at home. In a short time it had developed into a "Wartime Comradeship Committee" operating from the Central Office. Letters, newspapers and parcels went out from it to W.E.A. members at the front. W.E.A. friends visited those who returned as hospital patients. Mrs. Sanderson Furniss, a faithful friend and supporter of working-class interests in Oxford, came up to London and settled down as honorary secretary to the committee. With the help of Dorothy Jones and a team of voluntary workers, the committee's sphere of interest grew as the war effort grew. When the normal work of the Central Office ceased at the normal time, the work of the War Comradeship Committee would proceed into the longer evening hours.

By the end of 1915 it was clear that Mansbridge would have to lay down the burden of full-time office. His desperate illness had left its mark. He was able to do so with the satisfaction of a prophet who is allowed by providence to depart in peace having seen salvation. He had seen working-class education firmly hitched to the universities. He had seen the material expression of that significant merger, in the form of a great organization which had survived the shock of war conditions. He had carried his idea overseas and seen it take root and sprout in three great British Dominions. He had emerged from these efforts as an honorary graduate of his beloved Oxford University, a salaried director of the Co-operative Permanent Building Society, a member of the Board of Education's Consultative Committee and of much else—a seer who was invited to preach sermons in cathedrals, lecture in universities, and advise on educational projects of the most varied nature. Towards the W.E.A., the eldest child of his creative talent, he displayed some of the wisdom of the mother cat, who cherishes her kittens through their weeks of dependence, teaches them habits of cleanliness, usefulness and self-reliance, and having done so, renounces all desire to control the antics of the stripling kittens in favour of the eager assumption of new family responsibilities. This is not a perfect parallel, because unlike the cat, who is bored if not exasperated by the company of her adult progeny, Mansbridge retained a keen interest in the doings of the W.E.A. and presently reappeared as its vice-president. But he left his successors a completely free hand, and it was very soon clear that returning health brought a return of the creative urge in other directions: the National Central Library, the World Association for Adult Education, the British Institute of Adult Education, and the Seafarers' Education Service, which in 1938 developed into the College of the Sea—all these sprouted under his hands. The old magnetic influence was still at work. He could still make people do what he wanted. It was not, however, magnetic influence which in 1931 brought him into the honours list as a Companion of Honour, but a cool objective valuation by His Majesty's advisers of the contribution he had made to the educational vitality of the British Empire. The letters C.H. are not given lightly, nor can they be bought.

It was not easy to find an adequate successor for the office of General Secretary to the W.E.A. As a matter of general policy many people felt that as Mansbridge had tipped the balance of the Association on the side of the universities, it was now time to tip it on the side of the trade unions; and Mansbridge himself was of this opinion. It seemed that Mactavish was the man best able to do that. It was he who had spoken so effectively from the labour angle at a crucial moment of that vitally important Oxford conference in 1907. He knew the trade-union movement from the inside and spoke its language; and so, on February 19th, 1916, the Central Council of the W.E.A. unanimously confirmed his appointment. He took office at a difficult moment. The drain on W.E.A. personnel and the depletion of its classes had scarcely been arrested. The revival of its energies under the stimulus of external events in the educational world had scarcely begun. In the passage from her diary referred to above, Beatrice Webb describes Mactavish as a "blunt, energetic and somewhat commonplace Scot". History has certainly assigned him an uncomfortable place, his reign as General Secretary being sandwiched between those of two supermen, Mansbridge and Green, whose selfless devotion to the cause rendered them impervious to the temptations of the fleshpots. Mactavish was human, and perhaps in this respect "commonplace"; but if he had been all that much commonplace he would have remained a manual worker in the Portsmouth dockyard, instead of emerging from the rut to guide the W.E.A. through the remaining years of war conditions and the early years of post-war reconstruction. And energetic he certainly was, during those early war-time years of his reign.

According to T. W. Price,[1] the last piece of work carried through by Mansbridge as General Secretary of the W.E.A. was the revision of the constitution—somewhat overdue, owing to the postponement of the Annual General Meeting in 1914. The new proposals were based on seven years' experience of an awkwardly defined relationship between the districts and the centre, and of the operation as final authority over and above the Central Council, of an Annual General Meeting which all branch members, as well as representatives of branches and affiliated societies could claim to attend. The revised constitution abolished this cumbersome piece of machinery and substituted an Annual Convention whose function should be to receive a presidential address, discuss matters of educational policy, and "demonstrate the principles of the Association". The ultimate governing body was now to be the Central Council, representing the districts, the affiliated bodies and the national officers—the district secretaries being present without voting power. The Central Council was required to appoint an executive committee comprising one representative of each district and six representatives of affiliated bodies—again with the district secretaries in attendance. The Central Authority was no longer to recruit individual members but was to be financed by contributions from the districts and from nationally affiliated bodies; it was, however, empowered to raise funds on a national level. The government of the districts was to be in the hands of district councils representing the branches in the area and the locally affiliated bodies, together with one representative for every twenty individual members. This, in broad

[1] *The Story of the W.E.A.*, by T. W. Price, 1924, p. 56.

outline, was the new constitution. Its effect was to carry the W.E.A. a long way further than the 1907 constitution towards federal organization based on district autonomy. And head-quarters' finance was greatly simplified by the removal of responsibility for enrolling individual members at nominal subscriptions.

At the first war-time Annual General Meeting, held in Birmingham in October 1915, the new constitution was presented and, after a three hours' debate on forty-two amendments, was duly adopted. It was thus the last Annual Meeting to be held under the old 1907 constitution, whose expiry was fixed for May 30th, 1916. And it was the last to be graced by the presence of Mansbridge as General Secretary. What with that, and the growing casualty lists in the *Highway* and the stalemate on the Western front and the depletion of the tutorial classes, it was all rather sad.

Then came dawning realization of the paradox of modern war; and the relevance of that paradox was emphasized by the redefinition of objects in the new constitution, which imposed upon the W.E.A. the obligation to assist the development of a national system of education to secure for all the education essential for their "complete development as individuals and as citizens". That was a tall order in a free-price economy which had hitherto ensured that only a privileged few were in a position to achieve such "complete development". It would have been a tall order in time of peace when the deep springs of direct taxation were still untapped, the constructional industries not fully employed, and men's minds free to cultivate humane and civilized pursuits. It might have been a still taller order in time of war when man-power and materials were scarce, the tax-payer's endurance at full stretch, and the nation's thoughts directed to the efficient exercise of physical violence. It might have been, but it was not, and in this lies the paradox. Perhaps war imposes so great a military burden on the tax-payer that his back becomes accustomed to the load and a few millions more for the social services makes little perceptible difference. Perhaps the public consciousness becomes so accustomed to social changes, especially such changes as price control and rationing which make havoc of the time-honoured assumptions of a free-price economy, that familiarity breeds contempt—or at any rate acquiescence—at the thought of one change more. Perhaps when the higher values of mind and spirit are threatened by an upsurge of primitive violence they become so much the more precious, and the task of cherishing them is the more readily undertaken.

Both in regard to the position of women and the valuation of education this paradox of war became increasingly noticeable as the struggle with Germany dragged wearily on. Women shook themselves free of their trailing skirts and their frustrating taboos amid a chorus of popular adulation, at the very moment when the nation's survival depended primarily on the physical force and aggressive courage of men. At such a moment women secured recognition as citizens and a vastly expanded range for the exercise of their talents. And in the sphere of education the increasing war-weariness of the nation was marked by a new infusion of energy into the development of wider opportunities for the under-privileged. But that, of course, came later. At the outset things were not so good and education was thrown on to the defensive.

The assault came from the farmers. War service had depleted their agricultural labour force at a time when war needs made larger demands on their productive capacity. "From time whereof no memory is" the children of the countryside had worked in the fields, especially at fruit-picking and harvest time. They could do it again. What could be more healthy for them? This new-fangled book learning had always been an interruption—war requirements made it an even more absurd interruption. There was, indeed, some sense in the plea for relaxation of school attendance requirements under pressure of war needs. The Government was disposed to grant it—given safeguards and supervision. But the W.E.A. was very vigilant—here was the thin end of a destructive child-labour wedge. The matter was aired in the columns of the *Highway* and a memorandum was despatched to the Board of Education which had appointed a departmental committee to inquire into "the employment of children during the war".

In other directions the urgencies of war in its earlier phases were threatening the structure of national education. Some twenty thousand male teachers had volunteered for active service and an increasing number of women teachers were drawn into nursing, and later into the women's auxiliary services. Untrained personnel—highly gifted or sub-standard as the case might be—were drafted into teaching; schools and colleges were requisitioned for training or hospital purposes; women replaced men in boys' schools; the size of classes increased; and a wonderful excuse for educational economy was presented to those who had a natural inclination for that particular line of retrenchment. Even to those who had not it could well appear as a regrettable necessity.

The W.E.A. was disposed to take its expanded object very seriously indeed. Education, other than adult education, was not a wholly new preoccupation and one of its very earliest national conferences had been called for the purpose of initiating a demand for compulsory part-time education for adolescents. It had, however, played no significant part in the social reforming activities of the Liberal administration between 1905 and 1914 which had conferred upon education authorities the power to feed and the duty to medically inspect their school population. Now at last, it was deployed with all its fighting force on the widest possible education front.

On a Saturday afternoon in June 1916, the London District, under the energetic secretaryship of H. Goodman, convened a conference in the Farringdon Memorial Hall to consider the London County Council's proposal to effect a war economy of £360,000 on London education. Representatives of some three hundred trade-union, labour, and co-operative organizations attended. Temple presided. He was, he said, ready to credit the L.C.C. with good intentions but feared that this action might set a bad example throughout the country. Margaret Macmillan was no less charitably disposed. She thought that the L.C.C. had done its best, but was conscious of much misdirection of educational expenditure. Marion Phillips, of the Labour Party, was less charitable; and an amendment stiffening up the original resolution was moved by Herbert Morrison, of the National Union of Clerks, seconded by Susan Lawrence, a recent convert to Labour from Conservatism on the L.C.C., and carried. Two months later a similar conference of the

North-Eastern District, strongly supported by the Durham miners, was in full cry against educational economy.

Meanwhile, Mactavish was hard at work on a more positive task: the preparation of a comprehensive scheme of national education. A pamphlet entitled "What Labour wants from Education" was drafted and widely circulated among working-class and educational organizations. It indicated the questions requiring discussion and invited views on the direction of educational advance. When a committee of the W.E.A. set to work in September 1916, to draft an educational programme, it found widespread approval for the raising of the school age to fifteen and ultimately to sixteen, as well as for the institution of compulsory part-time education up to eighteen years.

On behalf of these, and other major reforms, an active campaign was launched. Up and down the country went Mactavish; district organizations were mobilized; conferences held; press publicity cultivated. Finally, at a culminating national conference of working-class and educational organizations on May 3rd, 1917, in the Central Hall, Westminster, the W.E.A. comprehensive programme was acclaimed and accepted. The public had now no excuse for underestimating the scope of the demands being made by responsible organizations. And it had been warned—for in the preceding year Temple had used his position as president of the education section of the British Association to demand free education for *all*, from elementary school to university.

It was, therefore, not surprising that in the same month as this culminating point of the W.E.A.'s campaign, Mr. H. A. L. Fisher, presenting his estimates as President of the Board of Education in the House of Commons, referred to a "quickened perception of the true place of education", foreshadowed considerable educational expansion in the near future, and secured a supplementary estimate of £3,856,000 from a generally sympathetic House. Indeed, the fact that H. A. L. Fisher was present to function in this ministerial capacity was in itself a sign that such "quickened perception" was astir in the Prime Minister. It had become a habit with Mr. Lloyd George to select "men of push and go" from the business world and entrust the relevant government departments to their care. It was an indication that he expected more abundant life from the departments concerned. When, therefore, he extracted the distinguished Vice-Chancellor of Sheffield University from his academic job, found him a parliamentary constituency and installed him at the Board of Education, one could only suppose that something really expansive was expected of that department, too.

On August 10th, 1917, Fisher introduced an Education Bill. It was no mean Bill; its proposals included, among other things, a general raising of the school-leaving age to fourteen, and the introduction of part-time continued education. But it fell short of W.E.A. demands and the *Highway* pronounced it to be "disappointing". There was worse disappointment three months later when the Government announced that the Bill would be shelved owing to lack of parliamentary time. The W.E.A. was not behindhand in expressing its disgust, but was assured by the Prime Minister that time would be given for a new Bill early in 1918. He was as good as his word.

The new Bill was no stronger than the old, but it was a Bill well worth having, and Fisher fought a strenuous parliamentary campaign on its behalf. He had attempted to stiffen the power of the Board of Education to coerce laggard local authorities and he had hoped to strengthen the local educational set-up by merging a number of small "Part III" authorities in their counties. On both counts local vested interests were too strong for him. But he secured his minimum school-leaving age of fourteen and he succeeded in a drastic curtailment of opportunities for child employment. To avoid the widespread practice of "marking time" in the top forms of the elementary schools, local authorities were required to provide central schools or classes for the older children. And their permissive powers were widely extended to include, among other things, a local school-leaving age of fifteen and the provision of nursery schools and classes—here was a limited triumph for Margaret Macmillan. On compulsory continuation schools Fisher was forced to compromise heavily—and here, indeed, one of the oldest and most cherished of W.E.A. demands was at stake. The section of the Bill requiring the provision of part-time education up to eighteen years was to come into force on two successive "appointed days". Later history relates that in spite of a strenuous campaign by Fisher himself, who really cared about his continuation schools, those days were never "appointed".

So the Bill became an Act, with all its possibilities and imperfections, and the name Fisher slips into its honourable place in the history of education beside the names Foster and Balfour—the earlier parents of notable parliamentary educational landmarks. But the Act was the beginning of trouble for the educational reformers outside Parliament because it left them with the piecemeal task of maintaining continuous pressure on local education authorities to ensure the widest possible use of their new and very considerable permissive powers. It was, however, a task for which the W.E.A. with its vigorous district organizations and its capacity for working its most energetic members into key positions in local government, was eminently well fitted.

The year which brought the Fisher Education Act and the Representation of the People Act with its inclusion of women in a greatly enlarged electorate, brought also the collapse of German armed resistance. On November 11th, 1918, at eleven a.m. the killing suddenly stopped. Some of the best young tutors, organizers and students of the W.E.A. had been among those killed. Tawney and Lowth had been nearly killed, but not quite. They slowly recovered from their wounds. The Association itself had come pretty near to the danger list, but could date its recovery from somewhere about the middle of 1916, for it seems to have been round about that time that the decline of membership, courage and hope gave place to renewed enthusiasm for the achievement of a brave new world, though there seemed to be nothing in the military situation to justify such optimism. At any rate, the end of the war found the Association with 219 branches, 2,526 affiliated societies, and 17,136 members—an increase in the number of branches and members as compared with 1914, and only a negligible decrease of affiliated societies. Tutorial classes had risen from their nadir of 99 to 121—not far short of the 145 operating in 1914—and the Government had increased its grant from £30 to £45 per class, thanks to pressure by the Central Joint Advisory Committee. The Oxford summer school had survived to complete its eighth successive year and there had been some considerable undertakings in the publishing line. In 1918 an *Education Year Book*, containing articles by, among others, Sidney and Beatrice Webb, had appeared as a W.E.A. publication. And W.E.A. cheap editions of Cole's *World of Labour* and Brailsford's *War of Steel and Gold* were the forerunners of other cheap editions of essential textbooks designed to solve the perennial problem of class students in hot competition for the same book at the same time.

Thus, restored to hope and vigour, the Association had conducted a full-scale educational campaign with some effect. Another lay ahead of it. In July 1917, the Government's Reconstruction Committee, which later gave place to the Ministry of Reconstruction, had appointed a sub-committee to report on adult education. Its composition reflected the prestige of the W.E.A. Tawney and Mansbridge were members of it. The Association's old friend and counsellor, A. L. Smith, now master of Balliol College, was its chairman. An analysis of its personnel shows eleven W.E.A. members, two adherents of the Central Labour College, and seven others. Arthur Greenwood and E. S. Cartwright were its secretaries. The end of the war found it still hard at work. So, too, was a committee appointed by the W.E.A. Central Council to report on rural education.

And now, once again, the cry went up at W.E.A. headquarters for more space and more money. In response to the first, a move was made in March 1918 from Red Lion Square to 16 Harpur Street. The new office had fourteen rooms—no less—but these had to be shared with the W.E.A. Book Department, the Central Joint Advisory Committee and the London District, now administered by Lowth as its district secretary. Dorothy Jones had retired after a long spell of strenuous service in the Central Office. Mrs. Hugh Dalton functioned as assistant secretary. Of course, more money was wanted because more space meant more activity.

In the summer of 1918 A. E. Zimmern retired from the gruelling job of honorary treasurer, the occupation of which was only one of his immemorial services to the W.E.A. He was succeeded by J. J. Mallon, at that time secretary of the Anti-sweating League, but soon to become Warden of Toynbee Hall. Seldom has an honorary treasurer combined so engaging an exercise of personal charm with a cheerful contempt for financial detail. His annual financial statements were a model of gay irresponsibility; but as honorary treasurer of the W.E.A. he had this advantage: like Mansbridge, though lacking Mansbridge's clearly visible aura of moral earnestness, he had a wide circle of friends and admirers. They could be found at Court, in the city, in university common-rooms, or in the sweat-shops of Whitechapel or Cradley Heath. And like Mansbridge, he could make people do what he wanted. With his eyes dancing and his own face crinkled with impish hilarity, he could make people laugh; but beneath the sparkle there was a warm friendliness and a profound concern for the under-dog. It takes a peculiar brand of humour to make a serious-minded audience laugh at a financial statement; and Mallon could do that—even when it was no laughing matter. However, things were not too bad in the summer of 1918, when it fell to the new honorary treasurer to launch an appeal for a W.E.A. Endowment Fund of £50,000. By the end of the year it had produced £2,466—not a bad start, all things considered.

The blessed word "reconstruction" had become familiar to hearers of speeches and readers of newspapers as Great Britain emerged from its preoccupation with the problems of war. It certainly inspired the active spirits of the W.E.A. as they faced the problems of peace.

# CHAPTER SEVEN

# THE STRUGGLE FOR THE TRADE UNIONS

THE winter which succeeded the defeat of Germany and ushered in the first post-war year was, for those whose lives were not disrupted and shadowed by personal bereavement, a time of exhilaration and hope.

It was not merely that the killing had stopped. It was not merely that the servicemen were coming home again after their bloody, muddy ordeal of trench warfare. There were more positive causes. The intractable problems of housing, local government, education, the status of women, the relations of employer and employed, were experiencing or about to experience a stimulating process of reconsideration in an environment from which fear of changing social patterns as well as fear of German aggression had been—or so it was widely believed—happily eliminated. Human expectation was perhaps a little inflated with a gas called "reconstruction", of luminous quality and somewhat lighter than air. But there were solid reasons for hope.

The W.E.A. enjoyed its share of expectation. It was indeed entering upon a new phase of its existence and the upheaval of the war and its aftermath was only part of the explanation of this newness. If there had been no war and no era of reconstruction it is fairly safe to say that round about the year 1918, W.E.A. history would have chronicled the end of one phase of activity and the opening of another—and this for the wholly satisfying reason that one vitally important job had been well and truly done and another, as yet scarcely attempted, was yet to do. The job done was the mobilization of the universities in the cause of working-class education, and Mansbridge did it—and having done it, passed from the immediate scene of his labours to other and allied activities. The job yet to be done was the mobilization of the working classes in the cause of their own education—but whether that job was in fact ever done, and if so precisely who did it, is a question less easily answered. This at any rate can be asserted: apart from the consolidation and expansion of its own organization, W.E.A. activities centred on two major tasks during the decade which followed the First World War. The first was the battle for general educational advance on the wide front of national and local politics. The second was the stimulation of an active educational response from the trade unions, and the formation of a dynamic consumers' demand for the kind of adult education which the founders of the W.E.A. had regarded as the key to power.

These three tasks—the expansion and improvement of the W.E.A. organization, the advancement of a comprehensive and equalitarian system of national education, and the educational crusade which demanded new close contacts with organized labour—were closely interlocked. The requirements of the trade unions demanded a new pattern of organization both locally and nationally. The gathering of forces to resist reaction and promote educational progress in the political field provided stimulating incentives for co-operation with organized labour. And both the political and the industrial crusade imposed new stresses and strains on the finances and administrative personnel of the W.E.A. It was indeed fortunate that the Association entered the stormy period of the Peace with its resources happily restored from the nadir of 1916, with its capacity as a political force established by its campaign on behalf of the Fisher Education Act, and with an infusion of new blood to constitute a second generation of W.E.A. enthusiasts.

Nothing could have been newer than the blood of G. D. H. Cole. Oxford had experienced its newness when in the years immediately preceding the First World War he used the opportunities presented by a research fellowship at Magdalen College to produce a challenging critique of the aims of British Labour. The Fabian Society experienced its newness when he dared to confront Mr. and Mrs. Sidney Webb with a Socialist philosophy which differed in certain fundamentals from the "gas and water" collectivism so deeply embedded in the programme of that organization. A German elder trade unionist named Sassenbach, who happened to be visiting

Oxford at this juncture, expressed intense surprise that such goings-on could occur "in the College at which the Crown Prince himself was studying". But Oxford, like the Kingdom of Heaven, comprised "many mansions", and in two of them Cole and Edward Prince of Wales were able to live peacefully as fellow inmates of Magdalen. Not that Cole was a peaceful person. His mind was like a very finely tempered sharp steel knife waiting for something to cut, and his appearance reflected his mind. And that mind, still further tempered by experience of war-time industrial problems, was in these post-war years at the disposal of the industrial Labour Movement. It was also at the disposal of the W.E.A. since he had good reason to know that education was necessary for the proper discharge of the responsibilities which lay ahead of the Labour Movement. He was thus eminently well qualified in collaboration with Mactavish, to take the initiative in an educational advance to the trade unions.

During the years which followed the war, trade-union officials had much to think about. They were nerve-racking, frustrating, and in many respects disappointing years. Behind the frustrations and disappointments—and perhaps in some measure because of them—a political Labour Party was, with recurrent set-backs, consolidating its power, snatching from the Liberal Party the status of "His Majesty's Opposition", and gaining the valuable experience of office—though as yet only of office unsupported by the power of a compact majority. That was to come. During the nineteen-twenties, however, one was more conscious of the set-backs than of the conquest of power. The steady decline of trade-union members from a record post-war figure of just over $6 \cdot 5$ millions to just under $3 \cdot 7$ millions in 1929 is significant. It marks two signal defeats on the industrial labour front: the collapse on "Black Friday", April 1921, of the "Triple Alliance" of miners, railwaymen and transport workers, and the defeat of the General Strike in 1926. In both cases the miners, balked of the nationalization recommended by a majority of the Sankey Royal Commission on the Coal Industry, were the principal victims of political reaction. But the whole industrial Labour Movement felt the strain and shared the bitterness as well as the depletion of trade-union funds—which last was assisted by the heavy demands of unemployment benefit. Indeed the shadow of unemployment brooded menacingly over the whole industrial Labour Movement. It was in the winter of 1920 that mass unemployment began to make itself felt. The unemployment percentage, now accurately gauged by the machinery of the 1920 Act, which extended national unemployment insurance to almost the whole range of industry, rose from 11 per cent in January 1921, to a high peak of 23 per cent in May of that year. It fell gradually to a mean monthly percentage of 10·2 per cent in 1924, but only in one year, 1927, was the corresponding figure less than 10 per cent. It rose to 15·9 per cent in 1930 and worse was yet to come. The extension of national unemployment insurance, the addition of dependents' allowances, and the concession of uncovenanted benefits for the long-term unemployed, mitigated the worst forms of hardship and degradation such as would dwell in the memories of those who had been dependent on the Poor Law during the depression of 1904. But the 'twenties ushered in no peaceful age of enlightenment in a "land fit for heroes", and tutors who dealt in economics and cognate subjects could observe a note of desperate urgency in the efforts of their trade-union students to understand the complex machinery in whose relentless cogs their destiny was engaged.

It was the Iron and Steel Trades Confederation which made the first constructive response to the educational blandishments of the W.E.A. Their assistant secretary, Arthur Pugh, knew Cole and Mactavish. Precisely who made the first proposal it is difficult to determine, but the courtship was effective, and it would be fairly safe to assume that Cole played a significant part as matchmaker. In October 1919, the Workers' Educational Trade Union Committee came into being, as a partnership between the two organizations, with Arthur Pugh of the Confederation as chairman, Arthur Greenwood of the W.E.A. as vice-chairman, and Mactavish and Wimble as secretary and assistant secretary. Its object was to administer funds contributed by the Confederation for the education of its members, and for this purpose the W.E.A., represented on the committee by Cole, provided the secretarial service both at headquarters and in the districts, where divisional committees following the pattern of the central committee were formed. The partnership was never intended to be monogamous. On the contrary a general invitation was issued to trade unions to come into the scheme, and this was quickly responded to by the Union of Post Office Workers and in due course by the Railway Clerks' Association, the Engineering and Shipbuilding Draughtsmen, and the National Society of Operative Printers and Assistants. By the end of the 'twenties, thirteen affiliated unions were represented on the W.E.T.U. Committee.

The W.E.T.U.C. conferred substantial benefits on its participating unions. While retaining control over their own educational schemes, the unions were able to make use of W.E.A. organization for starting classes, securing the services of highly qualified tutors and taking full advantage of grant-aided adult education—thus conserving trade-union educational funds for paying the class fees of their own students and financing scholarships and summer schools for their members. The W.E.A. was amply compensated for an increased load of administrative work by a development which expressed the original intention of its founders not merely to provide adult education of good quality for all and sundry, but specifically to provide for the working classes the kind of good quality education which they needed for a more abundant intellectual life—and not least for the effective use of the political power whose achievement was becoming a reality.

By the end of its first year, the Iron and Steel Trades Confederation was able to record a number of activities under W.E.T.U.C. auspices. It had provided several week-end and two special summer schools for Confederation members: eighteen members who were also tutorial class students had been given summer school scholarships; but this was not enough. On October 16th, 1920, Pugh assembled a conference of national trade-union representatives at the Steel Smelters' Hall in Gray's Inn Road, to discuss further steps for educational advance on the labour front. A resolution was passed calling upon the trade-union movement to meet the educational needs of its members, and approving the appointment of a committee of trade-union representatives to consider the best way of doing this, and report back to the bodies represented at the conference as well as to the Parliamentary Committee of the Trades Union Congress. A Trade Union Education Advisory Committee composed of national trade-union representatives, with Cole and Arthur Greenwood as co-opted members, thus came into being and set to work—the W.E.A. providing the secretarial assistance. In less than a year it had done what it set out to do—produced a report for the September meeting of the Trades Union Congress on "educational facilities for trade unionists". The report commended the machinery of the W.E.T.U.C. as a means of enabling trade unions to meet their educational needs by using the services of existing educational bodies, and indicated the universities, Ruskin College, the Labour College, and the W.E.A. as suitable agencies.

In the course of the committee's inquiry, Ruskin College, the Scottish Labour College, and of course the W.E.A., had furnished all the information asked for; but the Labour College and its associated body, the Plebs League, had stood sternly aloof. Indeed they had taken some pains to disassociate themselves from any traffickings with the university-tainted W.E.T.U.C. The Trades Union Congress, however, received the report sympathetically and resolved, on the motion of C. G. Ammon of the Union of Postal Workers, that the time having arrived for consideration of the educational needs of trade unionists, the General Council of the Trades Union Congress be instructed to co-operate with the Trade Union Education Enquiry Committee as to the best means of giving effect to its aims—"including", the resolution added, "the Central Labour College and Ruskin College".

Thus began a new era of educational activity on the part of the Trades Union Congress. In 1923 it created an educational fund with a maximum annual grant of £1,000 to assist working-class educational bodies approved by its General Council. In 1924 a Trades Union Congress Educational Advisory Committee came into being—on which the W.E.A. had two representatives. Bodies providing working-class education were invited to submit memoranda to it, and this time the Plebs were more responsive since the invitation had not come from the university-tainted W.E.T.U.C. The result of all this educational ferment was an agreement, ratified by the W.E.A. Central Council on May 16th, 1925, according to which working-class educational bodies declared themselves as prepared to accept the co-ordinating function of the Trades Union Congress, and to enter on a measure of joint action through a national committee of educational bodies under T.U.C. auspices. The agreement was in very general terms—it remained for the General Council of the Trades Union Congress to work out the joint committees of educational bodies foreshadowed by its terms. But the bodies concerned undertook to co-operate with one another and with the Trades Union Congress and to abstain from criticizing one another's good faith. This was significant because among those participating was the W.E.A.'s old enemy the Labour College, backed by the Plebs League with its monthly organ, *Plebs*.

To G. D. H. Cole, who had put much thought and effort into bringing trade-union education thus far, the Agreement of 1925 seemed to open "a new era in W.E.A. history", and one which would make intensified demands on the promotion of elementary and pioneer classes and the training of tutors to conduct them.[1] He was prepared to co-operate happily with the Labour College, for, he argued, there was surely a place for both in trade-union education. The Labour College was a propagandist body—propaganda had its place in the conquest of power by organized labour—only let it be recognized for what it was. The W.E.A. and the Labour College could, he thought, work very well together in their respective spheres. The W.E.A. had no quarrel with the Labour College or with its associated organization. Indeed one advantage of the new agreement under the auspices of the Trades Union Congress was that it was wide enough to include both movements, leaving it open to the trade unionist to choose between them.

In all this there is something strangely reminiscent of contemporary movements for Church unity and intercommunion. We seem to see Cole in the guise of a high-church Anglican

[1] See "The W.E.A. and the Future," by G. D. H. Cole; *Highway*, summer issue 1925.

pleading with the Vatican for Christian co-operation based on mutual recognition of one another's holy orders, and to hear echoes of the reply that such co-operation is possible only on the basis of Anglican submission to the One True Church. For this in fact was the Labour College attitude. As its adherent J. F. Horrabin put it, only to the extent that the W.E.A. accepts Labour College principles can there be any real co-operation under the Trades Union Congress scheme. Not that the adherents of the Labour College were constrained by any ecclesiastical decorum in their strictures of the W.E.A. The W.E.A. was condemned root and branch as a conspiracy subsidized by capitalists to dope the workers. Month by month attacks were launched in the columns of *Plebs*. The Carnegie Trust had, it asserted, decided to finance the publication of W.E.A. textbooks—let this be known! It was indeed true that the W.E.A. had accepted money—without conditions—from the Carnegie Trustees, for help in the supply of books, nor was there anything to prevent the inclusion of Marx's *Das Kapital* among the books supplied. And anyway, a refusal to handle books supplied with the help of Carnegie Trust funds would close the doors of many public libraries to supporters of the Labour College. Then there was the matter of trade-union membership. All Labour College tutors were trade unionists. The W.E.A. imposed no such condition on its tutors—shame on them! In fact, as the W.E.A. pointed out, the appropriate trade union for a teacher was a teachers' union, and W.E.A. tutors were members of the Association of Tutorial Class Tutors. Could the Labour College tutors say as much? They appeared to have no appropriate union at all. Nor did *Plebs* stop short of personal attack. During the General Strike of 1926, Temple had taken part in an effort to mediate in the long-drawn mining stoppage which followed the capitulation of the Trades Union Congress, as an alternative to the Churchillian policy of unconditional surrender. The Government was not pleased with this effort—nor was the Labour College; and under the heading of "Can You Wonder" *Plebs* accused him of withdrawing his name from a letter appealing for miners' relief. But perhaps the attitude of the Labour College to the W.E.A. is adequately summed up in the "Birthday Greeting" of *Plebs* to its sister organization on the occasion of the W.E.A.'s twenty-first anniversary in 1924:

Gentlemen—you ask us for a "birthday greeting". All we can say is that it is no fault of ours that you have reached your twenty-first anniversary: we should be much happier to attend your funeral.

Ever since our organization was founded there has been steady and necessary hostility between us. You exist to extend the benefits of university culture to the working man that you patronize. We show our readers that your education, and all education that is not based on the central fact of the class struggle, is false history and false economics. You hold out your hands for donations from employers; our funds come exclusively from the workers' own voluntary contributions. You claim to be above party, and your organization would collapse without its present plentiful subsidies from a capitalist state. Our education is directly intended to aid the workers in their emancipation from an outworn social tyranny, and we should esteem it a disgrace to become a dependent part of the instrument of that tyranny.

We note[1] with pleasure, in recent years, your decline and our rise. We note that gradual disinclination of capitalists to finance you as our propaganda exposes you and prevents you fulfilling their purpose. We note the formation of the "W.E.T.U.C."—a rabbit in a lion's skin—as a last effort of camouflage on your part, and thank you for the flattery it implies. We note, on our side, the phenomenal growth of Labour College classes, and the beginning at last, in spite of monetary difficulties that your salaried teachers cannot even imagine, of a series of truthful textbooks.

We hope and anticipate that when our "twenty-first birthday" comes—not so long now—we shall be able to celebrate also your complete disappearance.

Yours faithfully,
*for the Plebs Executive Committee,*
R. W. POSTGATE,
*Chairman.*

July 4th, 1924.

The proposition that extremes meet is nicely illustrated by a quotation from the *Morning Post*, contributed by A. D. Lindsay to the 1925 spring issue of the *Highway*. The W.E.A. is here referred to as part of " a vast subsidized machinery for the indoctrination of youth with a certain dogma and point of view, and for the equipment of street-corner orators with an armoury of phrases, catchwords, maxims and impressive passages from the works of Karl Marx and other Socialist orators".

How, it may be asked, did all this strike the ordinary trade

---

[1] This *note* is an odd hallucination since the number of W.E.A. students had risen from 5,320 in 1919 to 26,400 in 1924.

unionist for whose untutored mind the advocates of two opposing educational creeds were contending? It might be supposed that he was a little bewildered, as the common man is said by the advocates of Church reunion to be bewildered by the spectacle of warring Christian sects. It is more probable, however, that his interest was roused. The issue of *Plebs v. W.E.A.*, or as some would have it, propaganda *v.* education, was fought out on the floor of the Trades Union Congress. The W.E.A. was on its mettle for the defence of "how to think rather than what to think". Explanatory pamphlets were published and circulated. Some unions went one way—some another; but the W.E.A. had considerable achievements to show in the form of well-authenticated class records. It had its solid nucleus of three-year tutorial classes with their insistence on continuous application and quality of work, and its standards went beyond reliance on such booklets as the *Plebs'* "What to Read", in which the Webbs' *History of Trade Unionism* was presented as a "supplement" to a Plebs' *History of the Modern British Working Class Movement*, by W. W. Craik. The weakness of the W.E.A. lay rather in the shop-window presentation of its goods.

Needless to say, its trade-union campaign meant a lot of work, and early in 1925 a special propaganda committee was appointed for this particular effort. Pugh was its chairman, Lowth its secretary, and Muir, of whom more will be heard later, was its full-time national organizer. He initiated his campaign by visiting 83 towns and addressing 100 meetings— all of which, including the publication of a spate of pamphlets and leaflets, cost a lot of money and helped to land the W.E.A., at the close of 1925, with an overdraft of something over £497. But at long last education was a live issue in trade-union circles, and in the words of Arthur Pugh, the W.E.A. had come more and more "to think of workers' education in terms of working-class problems and working-class aspirations".

It had also more and more to think of workers' education in terms of what the State could or would do to maintain or expand its own national system, since this, after all, was one of its stated objects. The post-war era began well enough. Fisher was still at the Board of Education, and his 1918 Act had endowed local authorities with significant expansive powers. With the encouragement of a Board of Education circular a number of them immediately got busy on the preparation of schemes for the reorganization of their elementary education on the basis of central schools for the top forms. It was the business of the W.E.A., working through its district machinery, to ensure that such powers were fully used. That Fisher valued W.E.A. support in the operation of his Act was shown by the fact that he accepted an invitation to address the first post-war Annual Convention of the W.E.A. at Nottingham.

There were other auspicious new beginnings in this first post-war year. The tutorial class tutors, now a numerous as well as an academically distinguished company, met at Swanwick in Derbyshire and resolved themselves into the corporate personality of the Association of Tutorial Class Tutors—a body which subsequently proved its usefulness not merely by negotiating standard conditions of service, but by enabling its members to compare experiences and perfect the technique of teaching and discussion relevant to the needs of working-class students. A further contribution to those needs was made by the offer of Mr. and Mrs. Spalding, of Reading, to put their very lovely country house at the disposal of the W.E.A. for the training of tutorial class students as one-year class tutors and leaders of study circles. Thus residential summer schools at "Holybrook House", assisted by grants from the Board of Education and from the Cassel Trustees, became a feature of the W.E.A. year and one designed to realize the old aim of making the tutorial classes into what might be described as "seed beds" of educational activity. The Central Executive made itself responsible for the venture which it managed through a house sub-committee with T. W. Price, who had replaced Mrs. Hugh Dalton as assistant secretary, acting as Warden. In the following year a Working Women's College was instituted at Beckenham under Young Women's Christian Association auspices, and at Oxford, Ruskin College reopened after its war-time hibernation, with Sanderson Furniss as Principal and with the new feature of a hostel for women students. These last two developments, though not promoted by the W.E.A., nevertheless added to the feeling that adult education was on the march in a world which was really beginning to take it seriously.

In government departmental circles, too, the right ideas seemed to prevail. It was significant that when a Royal Commission on Oxford and Cambridge Universities was appointed in response to a cry to the Government for financial help from these ancient seats of learning, Mansbridge was made a member of it, thus ensuring that such matters as extra-mural work and intra-mural opportunities for working-class students would not be overlooked—nor in the end were they. And when the Reconstruction Committee's Sub-Committee on Adult Education, appointed in 1917, produced its final report in the summer of 1919, it was found to say all the right things, and to say them at very great length, about the development of adult education and the importance of the part played by voluntary organizations in its promotion. But this was scarcely surprising considering the preponderance of W.E.A. personnel on the committee itself, not to mention the fact that Arthur Greenwood and E. S. Cartwright were its joint secretaries. Indeed the usefulness of this report as a compendious descriptive textbook on adult education to date, quite apart from the usefulness of its recommendations, was considerable. There is a lot to be said for getting one's publications financed by H.M. Stationery Office.

Even outside the shores of Great Britain it seemed that adult education was on a flood tide, for in 1919 a World Association for Adult Education came into being, Mansbridge acting as midwife with Dorothy Jones in attendance. Mansbridge records the birth of this organization in his autobiography,[1] and relates it to his war-time educational contacts with dominion troops. It was, he explains, born in a teashop. But from such humble origins it rose meteor-like to the honour of President Masaryk of Czechoslovakia as its first president. The World Association proved to be a valuable disseminator of information and may in its turn be credited with two later examples of Mansbridgian proliferation: the British Institute of Adult Education and the Seafarers' Education Service.

[1] See *The Trodden Road*, by A. Mansbridge, pp. 96 *et seq.*

All things considered, therefore, there seemed to be good grounds for the exuberance of the W.E.A.'s Annual Report for 1919–20 which describes the growth of the Association during the period covered as "the most remarkable in its history". *Highway* circulation was up to pre-war level in spite of a price increase from a penny to twopence; tutorial classes had increased from 152 to 229; and student numbers had risen from 3,799 to 5,320. The barometer stood at set-fair—but not for long.

Early in 1921 a Cabinet instruction went out to all spending departments, among them, of course, the Board of Education, indicating that schemes involving expenditure not yet in operation, were to remain in abeyance. This was no bolt from the blue. The word "reconstruction" had already yielded pride of place to the word "economy". A Select Committee on National Expenditure had set forth the case for economy very forcibly in its Seventh Report. And all this meant the suspension of the Fisher Education Act with its promise of "appointed days". The green light which had shone from the Board of Education, turned suddenly to red with scarcely a pause on the amber.

On February 5th, 1921, over a thousand delegates of organizations interested in education assembled in the Farringdon Memorial Hall under the auspices of the London District W.E.A. C. G. Ammon of the Union of Post Office Workers presided, and Maude Royden, happily released from her preoccupation with the business of winning votes for women, moved a resolution of protest, which was carried in an atmosphere of scarcely suppressed rage. Up and down England the W.E.A. districts sprang to the defensive; but alas, the Government was not alone in its economy drive. Financial stringency at W.E.A. headquarters made it impossible to launch a national campaign comparable with its war-time effort in support of the Act whose effective operation was now menaced. And it had all happened so quickly. Only a year before, the W.E.A.'s Annual Report had recorded unprecedented progress. Now, in 1921, it had to admit that the Government's financial policy had "destroyed the new interest which the passing of the Act awakened, damped the ardour of educationists, and seriously weakened the chance of fitting the rising generation for the new duties which a changing world will impose upon them".

If educationists wanted to know precisely what their ardour had to overcome they had only to examine the proposals which the Committee on National Expenditure, under the efficient chairmanship of Sir Eric Geddes, had set forth in some detail. The school admission age was to be raised to six, the number of teachers, also their salaries and superannuation rights, were to be reduced. The school social services of meals and medical inspection, the provision of special schools for defectives, the grant of free places in secondary schools and state scholarships to universities, the number of teacher trainees, and the scale of secondary school maintenance allowances were all to suffer reduction. Secondary school and training college fees were to be increased, and also—this would naturally follow from the new staffing arrangements—the size of classes. It was calculated that the measures thus indicated would save some £36,000,000 in rates and taxes.

This was a little too much for Mr. Lloyd George's Government, with Fisher still at the Board of Education. There are no doubt limits to the ebb and flow of public opinion, though events in the political world make it difficult to maintain any confidence that this is so. The Government was not prepared to save £36,000,000 on the education of its future citizens, but it was prepared to save £55,000 on Board of Education estimates and a similar amount on rates. A spate of economy circulars descended upon local education authorities—they were not well received and were presently withdrawn in favour of a general warning of the Board's intention to limit expenditure. The result was a new outburst of anger by the W.E.A. and other education-conscious bodies. A great national protest demonstration was held on March 4th, 1922, and in many localities "Education Defence Committees" sprang into being. Meanwhile the teachers, having resolved that if economies had to be made they, rather than their children, should bear the brunt of them, offered and accepted a 5 per cent salary cut.

By the end of that year Fisher was out of office, and with a new Government came a new President of the Board: Edward

Wood, later to become Lord Halifax. It was a disappointing ending for Fisher's political career, but happily for him it was not his whole career, nor even the major part of his career: merely an interesting interlude in a far more satisfying career as teacher, historian and university administrator. The cloisters of New College, Oxford, received him gladly. He had lacked courage as a politician, and it was difficult to identify the man who had campaigned so ardently for continuation schools at the beginning of his political career, with the man who at the end of it was able to speak of the "sheer economic necessity" of letting children go out into "the University of Life" at the age of fourteen. But for one small mercy the W.E.A. had reason to be thankful in the year 1922–23. One of his last acts as President of the Board was to induce the Treasury to allow his department to except from the provisions of a restrictive circular "classes conducted solely for the liberal education of adults".

The change of government in the autumn of 1922 seemed to offer little hope of any major relaxation in the economy drive, except that the *Highway* was able to note the appearance of many good friends of education in the newly elected House of Commons—though its inclusion among them of Oswald Mosley showed a perspicacity inferior to that of Beatrice Webb, whose first impression of him was that: "So much perfection argues rottenness somewhere". However, the new President of the Board of Education was a man of genuine culture and, so far as domestic politics were concerned, of high principle. Early in 1923 he was able to convey to a deputation organized by the W.E.A. and led by Temple his hope that the limit of financial restrictions on education had been reached. But fate allowed him no time to show whether he could encompass better things; for in the following year another General Election brought Labour into office for the first time, though without the effective power of a clear majority. But with Charles Trevelyan at the Board, came the promise of "a great expansion of secondary education", and it looked as though the tide had turned at last.

And so indeed it had. For though Charles Trevelyan had as ephemeral a sojourn at the Board as his Conservative predecessor and was succeeded in 1924 by Lord Eustace Percy, and

though Lord Eustace at the outset of his reign declared to a
W.E.A. deputation that he could not contemplate raising the
school-leaving age to fifteen because it would add £2,700,000
to the rates, nevertheless a new, powerful weapon was
presently put into the hands of progressive educationalists.
In 1926 a report by the Board of Education Advisory Committee on the Education of the Adolescent, presided over by
Sir Henry Hadow, was published. This document, known to
history as "the Hadow Report", comprised a well-argued plea
for universal secondary education starting with an educational
break at the age of eleven plus, and for the raising of the
school-leaving age to fifteen in order to make such secondary
education really worth while. Here then was a programme
backed by an influential official publication, and one which,
even without a statutory increase in the school-leaving age,
enabled progressive local education authorities to get on with
the reorganization of their schools on Hadow lines within the
framework of their existing statutory powers. To such development the Board itself was favourably disposed, and the W.E.A.
was presented with a constructive programme of action on its
various local fronts—particularly those on which W.E.A.
members were occupying strategic positions as members of local
education committees. Meanwhile, public opinion was definitely
on the move as regards the raising of the statutory school-
leaving age. The Hadow Report had made and publicized an
unanswerable case. It is interesting, though not perhaps
surprising, to find the names of Mansbridge and Tawney in
the list of Hadow committee members.

One achievement of particular moment to the W.E.A. can
be identified with Labour's first year of office: the framing of
a comprehensive code of Adult Education Regulations for the
administration of government grants. Here at last was an
attempt to define and systematize the Board's financial
responsibility for extra-mural adult education provided by
universities, as well as for that provided by approved voluntary
bodies such as the W.E.A., and the regulations involved the
recognition of a distinction between the adult education
functions of these two agencies. That provided by universities
comprised preparatory and tutorial classes, extension courses

and tutorial class vacation courses. That provided by approved associations, which made less demand upon the students, comprised terminal and one-year courses and vacation courses organized for their students. For each type of course detailed requirements were set forth as a condition of grant-aid.

The 1924 Adult Education Regulations marked an important stage in the development of the W.E.A.'s relations with the Board of Education. For the W.E.A. they meant a raising of the standard of class work, and a widening of class activities, an improvement in tutors' salaries, and, in view of the complications incidental to a new and complicated financial regime, valuable opportunities for personal contact between the district secretaries and the Board's officers, which doubtless contributed to the higher education of both. But they had their dangers. The new regulations provided the Board with a motive for economizing administrative costs by encouraging local education authorities to take its place in grant-aiding W.E.A. classes and this, in 1925, became its declared policy. It was not a policy that the W.E.A. liked. Local education authorities, especially the more reactionary county authorities, were on the whole less capable than the Board's officers of understanding the aims and nature of W.E.A. class work—they had a better understanding of the evening institute and vocational class work which was familiar to them. Certainly any such development was unlikely to secure the uniformity of standard at which the new regulations were aimed—quite the contrary. Only the supporters of *Plebs* really appreciated the possibility of seeing the local education authorities in financial control of W.E.A. classes, since this would complicate the old firm partnership between the workers, the universities and the Board of Education. Clearly here was a matter calling for tact and vigilance on the part of the W.E.A.

For the exercise of both these qualities the experience of this post-war decade provided the Association's officers with ample opportunity. They had to manipulate a bewildering range of human contacts. They had to deal with civil servants, politicians, local authorities, students, tutors, branch members, vice-chancellors, trade unionists and the Press. From mastering the intricacies of high finance they had to turn to repelling the crudities of low abuse. And there came a time when tact was required for internal use in connection with what the Annual Report describes as Mactavish's "continued ill-health", leading to his resignation in 1928, with a year's sick leave, on full pay, and a pension after that if he was unable to take up other work. The Association certainly owed him a permanent debt of gratitude for his war-time services and for his energetic, sympathetic and effective approach to the trade unions during its crucial reorientation of W.E.A. policy. But his increasing resort to alcoholic stimulants meant increasing tension in the Central Office, and it is scarcely surprising that the Annual Report of the preceding year describes the period covered as "in some respects the most trying through which our Association has passed for a number of years".

His place as General Secretary was taken by J. W. Muir, who had in fact functioned as "Acting General Secretary" for nearly a year before the final break with Mactavish. Muir must indeed have had a difficult time, but he had wide experience with which to encounter difficulties—first as a Clydeside shop steward at a time when industrial conditions in that area were turbulent, later as a Clydeside M.P., and later still as Parliamentary Secretary to the Ministry of Pensions in the short-lived Labour Government of 1923–24, after which he lost his seat. Contact with Cole, in connection with the Guild Socialist Movement, had led to his interest in the W.E.A. and his advent, to begin with, as national organizer, brought a new link with organized labour. He was universally liked and trusted, and it was a personal as well as an administrative tragedy for the W.E.A. when, having survived the discomforts of Mactavish's decline and fall, reorganized the office and got all its work well in train, he was obliged, at the end of 1929, to undergo a dangerous operation which failed to save his life.

And through all these years, here and there with set-backs, but like an incoming tide whose waves advance a little, recede a little, but in the end advance—the W.E.A. was spreading its activities and extending its organization. One result was that it again outgrew its constitution, which had to be amended in 1923 to make definite provision for the inclusion on the

Central Executive of representatives of the various national co-ordinating working-class bodies—including, of course, the W.E.T.U.C.

Meanwhile there were administrative developments both at the centre and in the districts. At the centre, the old book-room was expanded in 1922 into the Students' Bookshop and launched into independent existence as a limited company with Sir William Beveridge as chairman of its board of directors, and the Central Executive as holder of its ordinary shares. A less successful venture was the establishment in 1928 of a Bureau of Public Education at the Central Office. It was hoped that teachers' organizations and other educational bodies would co-operate in support of this department which would serve them all as a centre of information and a producer of useful publications. This support was, unfortunately, not forthcoming; but the W.E.A. acted alone. The Bureau came into being, and with Miss Simeon as secretary did some useful work. Publications, however, were already flowing in an increasing stream from the W.E.A., and with the help of the Tutors' Association, study "Outlines" appeared from 1926 onward. It is interesting to note that a somewhat indifferent demand for these "Outlines" by W.E.A. students was amply compensated by large orders from secondary schools.

Out in the districts a decline in the numbers of classes and students in 1927—the first recession for many years—stimulated new efforts at organization. Area committees with voluntary organizers came into being within the district organizations, for the purpose of helping the more isolated branches, and organizing "Saturday schools" where single branch organization was weak. Meanwhile there were a number of constructive developments in district organization. In 1929 the Yorkshire District became so unwieldy as a single organization that a new district, South Yorkshire, was carved out of it and given separate existence. And in a similar manner the Southern District hived off a new district for the three counties of Oxfordshire, Buckinghamshire and Berkshire. Two more district developments deserve special mention.

The first, in time, is the evolution of the North Staffs organization which came into existence as a full-blown W.E.A.

district in 1921. It could claim direct descent from the historic Longton tutorial class which had acquired pioneer status by virtue of the fact that its first meting was on the Friday preceding the Saturday on which the Rochdale class first met. The Longton class, it will be remembered, gave birth to an educational campaign, inspired by E. S. Cartwright, in six neighbouring mining villages. By 1920 the six centres had become 28, with 630 students, and work was carried on in the name of the North Staffs Miners' Higher Education Movement. It was, in effect, the W.E.A. of North Staffs, and with financial help from its local education authorities and the Oxford Joint Committee for Tutorial Classes, it was able to secure a full-time organizer and a resident tutor; by which time a more all-embracing title was required and it became the North Staffs Adult Education Association.

The second development was somewhat more complicated. It concerned Scotland, whose separate national educational set-up suggested the need for a separate Scottish approach to the organization of adult education. The history of the W.E.A. in Scotland begins with a visit by Mansbridge, somewhere about 1910, to preach the gospel of adult education in Glasgow. The Trades Council of that city heard him gladly and a provisional committee was formed. But his message, like the seeds in the Gospel of St. Matthew, fell in stony places, "and because they had no root they withered away". By 1911 this ephemeral organization was no more. But some classes continued to work on W.E.A. lines and so produced the nucleus of a branch organization in 1915. Meanwhile Edinburgh formed a branch in 1912, and by the end of the First World War, Aberdeen, Ayrshire and Dundee had followed suit. In 1916 a Scottish Provisional Council came into being which kept W.E.A. work alive, and in 1919 it was fully constituted and furnished with a full-time organizing secretary whose salary was guaranteed by the Central Council. Within a very short time all four Scottish universities and a dozen local education authorities were contributing financially to Scottish W.E.A. activities, though dependence on the Central Council continued for some time to be a feature of Scottish W.E.A. finance. In 1921 the first Scottish summer school was held, and in 1922 the Scottish

W.E.A. was solvent. It ceased to be solvent in the following year, but that, the Central Council generously admitted, was due to expansion of work rather than a diminution of Scottish generosity. Work in Scotland expanded, and Muir, as an ex-Clydesider, gave it special attention in his capacity of national organizer. But whatever the Clydeside may have felt, the Edinburgh branch found itself unable to remain part of an Association which could ratify an educational agreement with the Trades Union Congress and thus—it was alleged—compromise its political independence. On January 8th, 1926, the Edinburgh branch decided by a majority of 54 votes to 10 to secede from the W.E.A. and form a new organization. This action came as a considerable surprise to the W.E.A. Executive —the more so because the Scottish branches had been invited to discuss the T.U.C. agreement before the Scottish W.E.A. Council approved it—prior to its final approval by the W.E.A. Central Council. No branch had then indicated disapproval. But as a result of the secession statements flew backwards and forwards. Had the W.E.A. changed its policy? Of course it had not. Was the unbiased nature of its classes assured? Of course it was. The Scottish local education authorities, whose financial help was in question, had to be assured of that, and in the end most of them were—but not all.

Through all this post-war decade—in major respects so encouraging because in spite of its set-backs the workers were on the road to power and the usefulness of an Association which offered a key to its use was unquestionable—one uncomfortable preoccupation remained: finance. To an increasing extent, educational trusts were prepared to put money into W.E.A. hands for special purposes, knowing that it would be well used: the Gilchrist Trust, the Thomas Wall Trust, the Carnegie Trust, the Cassel Trust. And to an increasing extent university money, taxpayers' money and ratepayers' money flowed through W.E.A. hands. Contributions for the provision of education and the initiation of educational projects were thus readily forthcoming. But contributions for the organization to support these expanding activities were not. In 1920 a deficit on the year's working of £2,491 was partly met by drawing on the National Endowment Fund; but only partly, and a deficit of £957 remained. Things were better in 1921 owing to strenuous efforts by the honorary treasurer and a contribution to the general funds of £150 a year for four years by the Gilchrist Trust. Things were better—but not for long, and the dream that financial support should and could come from working-class organizations remained unrealized.

Such thoughts did not, however, damp the enthusiasm with which in the summer of 1924 the W.E.A. celebrated its twenty-first birthday at a coming-of-age convention in the city of its official birth, Oxford. Its natural birth had, it may be remembered, occurred some months earlier in a little parlour in the neighbourhood of Clapham Common. It was a heartening celebration, enlivened by greetings from kindred organizations—that from *Plebs* came, unfortunately, too late for inclusion but was published subsequently in the *Highway*.

There was, however, one matter for regret in these rejoicings. Temple, who had in 1922 become Bishop of Manchester, found that episcopal duties in the north were incompatible with presidential duties in the south—at any rate with presidential duties as he interpreted them, since he was not, and had never been, a mere figurehead president. He had given the Association sixteen years of wise leadership covering the formative period of its concordat with the university world from which he came and in which he had his intellectual roots. Now that this concordat was about to be reinforced by a concordat with the Trades Union Congress it was thought fit that the office of president should pass to one who had his roots in the world of organized labour. So Fred Bramley, one of the principal architects of the Trades Union Congress General Council, was elected in his place, and nobody would have guessed from Bramley's cheerful and forceful inaugural speech that in little more than a year he would be no more. His death was a bad blow to wider circles than the W.E.A., for whose presidency Arthur Pugh was an obvious and worthy successor: Arthur Pugh—whose union had initiated the first educational partnership with the W.E.A. away back in 1919, and who had been the W.E.A.'s leading ambassador in trade-union circles ever since. But Pugh's term of office was scarcely longer than Bramley's, though for a happier reason. In 1928 pressure of trade-union work called him away, and Tawney was elected as his successor.

From university leadership the Association had swung over to trade-union leadership. With Tawney it seemed to choose a middle way. For with all his university roots and subsequent academic eminence, Tawney had since his undergraduate days enjoyed far more intimate contacts with working-class organizations than Temple. He had played a leading part in the struggle of the miners for nationalization; he had contested a parliamentary election as Labour candidate; and why Ramsay MacDonald did not make use of his services when Labour accepted office in 1923 is best known to Ramsay MacDonald. What Tawney had meant to the W.E.A. in its earliest days has already been related; he was now to be its principal interpreter to the world at large and to itself, and his message to the *Highway* in his first year of office indicated that he was no evader of uncomfortable issues. Where the W.E.A. was weak, complacent or foolishly optimistic, the truth was going to be told. He was aware of its achievements: 459 branches, 16 district organizations, 11,750 tutorial class students, 19,000 terminal and one-year class students, and joint committees in every university, that was no mean effort for a quarter of a century's work. No less an achievement was the general recognition that "the miner, the engineer and the weaver need humane education as much, and can turn it to as good account, as the barrister or civil servant"—a view that in 1903 was a paradox and in 1928 a commonplace. But "unless it is to relapse into the melancholy conditions of a society poring with senile satisfaction over the statistical records of its past achievements", the W.E.A. must . . . really there seemed no end to the things that it must do. And incidentally it must realize that "the educational activities of the Association have grown out of all proportion to its finance and organization".

Much was going to be required of the W.E.A. under its new president, including a brain-racking effort of self-criticism.

# CHAPTER EIGHT

# THE W.E.A. LOOKS AT ITSELF

SOMEWHERE about the year 1922 an ex-service Ford utility van, the property of the Young Men's Christian Association, and known to her familiars as "Black Maria", was chugging over the lower slopes of the Cotswolds with a W.E.A. lecturer *en route* for an evening class. It was one of many kind services performed by Black Maria (by permission of her masters) in the cause of rural education. Sometimes she would carry several lecturers, dropping them complete with impedimenta of lantern slides or film strips at lonely village halls, and rounding them up at the evening's close for the return drive to Oxford whence these activities proceeded. But on the night in question there was only one passenger. As Black Maria throbbed and panted up and over the crest of a Cotswold curve the moon rose; and there clearly defined against the night sky to the south were the gigantic steel masts of the Leafield wireless installation. Both driver and lecturer noticed the phenomenon. In the driver it provoked a train of thought. Presently he remarked: "In a few years' time I shan't need to drive you to your lectures. You'll be sitting at home in your study doing your stuff, and the students will be taking notes by their own firesides." The lecturer thought this rather nonsense—as indeed it was, but not quite such nonsense as the lecturer thought. For in 1924 Temple's address as retiring W.E.A. president was broadcast by the B.B.C. from the Sheldonian Theatre, Oxford, and two years later a W.E.A. resident tutor, D. A. Ross, was on the air with a course of lectures on "One Hundred Years of Working-class Progress". By which time the B.B.C. was committed to "education" as one-third of its function; and as the W.E.A. Annual Report for 1929 records, "The Adult Education work of the B.B.C. is developing rapidly". The Central Council for Broadcast Adult Education had been set up, conferences on adult education had been called by the B.B.C. in various parts of the country, and the W.E.A. was co-operating in what promised to be a potent new engine of intellectual uplift, locally through its district councils and at the centre by the presence of its General Secretary on the B.B.C.'s Adult Education Committee.

There was much that the W.E.A. could do for the educators at Broadcasting House. Indeed, there was much that they could do for one another. The B.B.C. could engage the world's most eminent lecturers and pay them fees beyond the dreams of education departments or university joint committees. The W.E.A. could, or so it believed, assemble the listeners at the receiving end, provide the leadership to focus their minds on what they heard and get them talking about it. Such was the pattern of the "wireless discussion group" for which the 1929 W.E.A. Annual Report claimed many successes. Only in North Wales do there appear to have been doubts, since, as was explained on behalf of that district, "such groups were only successful where a very well-qualified group-leader was present" and "in these circumstances the need for a wireless lecture is not great".

Seldom has the exhaustion of a good hope been so strenuously resisted as was the good hope that men and women might be persuaded to cultivate socially the educational opportunities provided by the B.B.C. North Wales had diagnosed its mortal disease at the moment of its first flowering. For successful group listening you must have a group-leader who can add something to the discussion; otherwise, why leave your own fireside to join a group. He must be expert enough to be a W.E.A. lecturer on the subject under discussion. And if he then "does his stuff", effectively *hey presto*, you have a W.E.A. lecture with all the effort of organization and grant-aiding necessary to produce one. It took ten years to convince the B.B.C. and the co-operating adult education organizations that this was so. Nor was the lesson learned until much money had been spent by the B.B.C. on councils, conferences, travelling expenses, and training schemes for potential group-leaders. Many man-hours, too, had been spent by the officers and members of educational organizations, but this was less to be regretted since they had for the most part greatly enjoyed their incursions into the unfamiliar world of broadcasting, both at

Portland Place and in the B.B.C. Regions. Moreover, personal contact with the officials of the B.B.C. engendered the conviction that the great corporation under its austere chief Sir John Reith really meant business when it accepted "education" side by side with "information" and "entertainment" as its threefold task.

On the face of it, apart from the failure of group-listening, adult education appeared to be in spate. Towering above all other cultural agencies rose the B.B.C. with its high principles and its gigantic resources. The days when the Manchester University Settlement had loaded its piano on to a milk-float and trundled it through the slums in order that the denizens of those mean streets might catch an echo of great music, were gone. From the curtained windows of these same streets would blare the works of the world's finest composers, beautifully performed, if, perhaps, a little over-amplified. Or it might be the authentic voice of Russell or Eddington, Temple or Gielgud, speaking grace and wisdom to the multitude.

Meanwhile, in their own small ways, voluntary bodies were exploiting for educational ends their direct contacts with human beings. The Young Men's and Young Women's Christian Associations were busily expanding their educational work. So were the Adult School Union, the new community centres, and the educational settlements; and in the country the Rural Community Councils and the Women's Institutes. One might add the spectacular expansion of amateur drama encouraged by the British Drama League—a very magnetic instrument for bringing men and women together for the pursuit of cultural ends. "There have been ages", said Tawney, in his 1933 Presidential Address, "in which the inaccessibility of information to the mass of mankind was a major problem. Our own is not among them. From rosy morn to dewy eve, through the eye and through the ear, we are inundated with materials for making up our minds. What we appear to lack is a mind to make up."

These were dangerous years for the W.E.A., the more so because neither the competing influences nor the great depression of the early 'thirties appeared to affect human response to its ministrations. It is true that it never succeeded, in spite of periodic exhortations, in substantially raising the proportion of class members who were prepared to join the Association and take an interest in its missionary work. But class membership flourished, and after a period of stagnation, W.E.T.U.C. activities showed notable signs of expansion after 1933. This, combined with effective moves for educational partnership with the Co-operative Movement and the Club and Institute Union, would seem to suggest that the strenuous efforts made during the 'twenties to direct W.E.A. activities to the needs of working-class organizations had achieved a considerable measure of success—and so indeed they had. But it was not the kind of success that can be precisely measured in statistical form, or that is likely to remain unaffected by the shifting currents of social and economic change. Look to your standards; look to your class composition; put not your trust in statistics; the larger the scale of our operations the more we should look to the quality of our students; "of all forms of educational superstition the worship of statistics is the least intelligent"; "our business is not to be the educational Woolworth of the day"— such were the annual presidential exhortations which prompted the editor of the *Highway* to remark that "Mr. Tawney's pronouncements have the qualities of St. Paul's Epistles to his errant flocks".[1] But he was not content with unspecified warnings. Was the proportion of manual workers falling? He suspected that it was. And what of the tutors? It is to be feared that the qualifications, of a small minority doubtless, were "not such as would have caused them to be accepted in the past".

Tawney's was not the only warning voice. Cole, too, was in a soul-searching mood, but his searches led in a different direction. He was less concerned with academic standards—more with the possibility that not enough was being done to meet the needs of less advanced, less systematic students. In the old days the branches busied themselves with the provision of popular lectures;[2] the day for that was past. Others were doing it and could do it better. Informal class-work and discussion was what the W.E.A. can do—should do—and how many of those who go out from the tutorial classes were doing it? But his particular fear was that the W.E.A.[3] might become a sort of universal

[1] See *Highway*, March 1936.    [2] *Ibid.*, September 1930.    [3] *Ibid.*, March 1931.

provider of adult education at the expense of concentrating on working-class education. This, of course, was a growing fear and likely to grow yet more as changes in the social and economic structure tended to make havoc of class distinctions. But that time was not yet, and the resident tutor at Bacup raised solemn thoughts when he diagnosed in that bleak industrial area a tendency for the W.E.A. to become a middle-class organization: a failure of the W.E.A. to attract industrial workers.

These, of course, were general statements and redounded to nobody's discredit. It was otherwise with a complaint raised in the *Highway* of March 1935, by an article entitled "This Grant-grabbing Racket". Its author was H. A. J. Martin, himself a tutorial class tutor and a former W.E.A. student. It might be presumed that he would know his facts, and very possibly he did—but they were not palatable facts, nor were they judiciously presented. His article comprised a general assertion that class registers were habitually falsified in order to comply with grant conditions, this with the connivance of tutors who feared for their salaries, students who wished to evade written work, and officials who gloried in satisfactory statistical returns. Such an indictment could not be ignored. An immediate reply came from the secretaries of the Cambridge Joint Committee under whose auspices Martin worked, and whose tutors gravely resented this indiscriminate imputation of dishonesty. But the matter roused widespread discussion and, of course, had to be investigated.

The Central Executive Committee accordingly appointed a sub-committee for this purpose. Its report admitted occasional lapses but failed to sustain the sweeping charge implied by Martin's use of the words "racket" and "virtual conspiracy". A tangible result of its work was a W.E.A. publication: *Aims and Standards in W.E.A. Classes*. There can be little doubt that Martin overstated his case—perhaps deliberately for the purpose of forcibly directing attention to what might have developed into a serious relaxation of academic standards. If so, he performed an important service—though in such a, way as to get small thanks for it.

There was, however, one indictment against adult education as a whole which could not be disputed—and this was summed up in 1932 by a Board of Education report on "Adult Education and the Local Authorities" in the word "unsystematic". The report diagnosed confusion of standards, a disproportionate growth of less intensive courses, and an urgent need for the planning of local schemes to secure effective partnership between the voluntary and statutory purveyors of adult education. Here, indeed, in the demarcation of function as between the local education authorities and the W.E.A. was a problem which was assuming increasing proportions. It was not the only one.

The nineteen-thirties had begun well enough for educational enthusiasts, provided they kept their eyes glued to the political scene and ignored the trend of industrial and trade statistics. A Labour Government was in office, and though the question of the school-leaving age had been regrettably absent from the King's Speech in the summer of 1929, an early announcement was made that the Government intended to legislate. A Bill raising the leaving age to fifteen was introduced in December 1929, but no date was given for its second reading and the W.E.A. mobilized its well-oiled machinery of propaganda by conference and pamphlet, in close collaboration with the National Union of Teachers. When the Government announced that the Bill would be dropped and a new Bill substituted, agitation continued. Confidence in Ramsay MacDonald's educational intentions wore very thin—the more so when in June 1930 the second Bill was dropped. But a third promised better success: introduced in October 1930, it survived all its stages in the House of Commons, only to be rejected in February 1931 by the House of Lords with, according to J. J. Mallon, "a levity and callousness which aroused the deepest resentment". It was in vain that the Government promised speedy reintroduction in order that the measure might be forced through under the Parliament Act, since the Government itself failed to survive the financial crisis of that same year, and by the end of it a General Election conducted in an atmosphere of panic, had installed in power a Government pledged to economy on all that made life worth living for the working classes, whose spectacular swing to the right had guaranteed it a powerful working majority.

It is on record that Ramsay MacDonald, who figure-headed the new administration, wept for education. He deeply sympathized with its ideals and regretted, "no one more", that even education could not be spared from the general sacrifices required by the financial emergency as revealed in budget deficits.

By this time the country was in the trough of a trade depression which landed the Unemployment Insurance Fund in a debt of £115,000,000 and drove the unemployment percentage to the record figure of 22·8 in August 1931. Among the W.E.A.'s attendant preoccupations was the problem of what educational service it could render to the unemployed. This was no new preoccupation. As early as 1927, Alice Cameron, an experienced tutorial class tutor under the Oxford Joint Committee, had initiated under W.E.A. auspices at Lincoln an experimental workshop for the unemployed of that city, in the hope that other W.E.A. branches might follow Lincoln's example, and that a national policy might eventually take shape. The experiment did indeed attract widespread interest and served as a model for the activities of other agencies for unemployed relief. But the W.E.A. worked for the most part on lines more familiar to its organization. It promoted summer schools for the unemployed, and in co-operation with the Trades Union Congress Education Committee it provided classes and lectures for organizations of unemployed workers. The keynote of its policy was, however, to get unemployed men and women to join the normal classes rather than to segregate them on the basis of their common misfortune. And in due course, the optimistic belief that unemployment might encourage educational studies by providing the leisure, normally lacking, for reading and essay writing, gave place to the knowledge that nothing good can come of unemployment—nothing. For even unlimited leisure, when shadowed by anxiety and resentment, is not conducive to intellectual concentration or objective thought.

The major task, however, which the depression and the collapse of Ramsay MacDonald's Labour Government set the W.E.A. was in the field of public education. It was obvious from the outset that education would bear the full force of the economy blast which produced the household means test and the cuts in unemployment benefit. It was for the W.E.A. with its accumulated experience of two previous anti-economy campaigns to take the field against what promised to be an even more formidable assault on educational standards with a fierce blaze of popular panic behind it. The assault came on a wide front. There were to be cuts everywhere and a general slowing down of educational progress. But the most vicious attack was directed against secondary education. Free places were to be restricted and a means test attached to maintenance allowances, and Board of Education Circular 1421 carried this doleful directive to local education authorities.

The challenge was met. From W.E.A. headquarters instructions went out that branches were to summon meetings—organize conferences of working-class and educational bodies, send protests to the Prime Minister, to the President of the Board of Education, to the local Member of Parliament. They were to distribute leaflets, make contact with W.E.A. members on the local education committee—agitate, agitate, agitate! Three times this same task of agitation had been imposed on the W.E.A. and each time it responded, it responded more effectively, more influentially, than the time before. Its officers had become past-masters in the art of resisting educational economies.

It almost seemed as though the economizers had become past-masters in the audacity of their suggestions. The Committee on Local Expenditure set up by the Government under the chairmanship of Sir William Ray went so far as to consider the imposition of fees in elementary schools, only to dismiss it on the ground that the attendant means test would be difficult to implement. But it was fertile in suggestions for economies on school meals and medical services. £15,000, for instance, could be saved if fewer tonsils were removed. There were further opportunities for economy in the closing of redundant schools, and the reduction of teaching staffs. Meanwhile, variations in local expenditure on education suggested that some authorities were spending more than the bare minimum—this should be inquired into.

There was one economy of more intimate concern to the

W.E.A. It was unlikely that the Board of Education's grants for adult education could escape the general massacre; nor did they. With the advent of a Labour Government in 1929 it had looked as though the way were open for an improvement in the existing Board of Education grant regulations. In collaboration with the Central Joint Advisory Committee proposals for revision were hammered out, followed by negotiations with the Board which resulted in the Amended Regulations of 1931. University joint committees were henceforth allowed to appoint a limited number of full-time tutors for work of a pioneer character, provided that each of them undertook at least one tutorial class. The W.E.A. would have liked the concession to apply to other than university bodies— nevertheless, such as it was, the revision was an important one, and the fact that it was conceded at the suggestion of the W.E.A. was a tribute to the excellent relations which had been built up through two decades between the W.E.A. and the senior officials of the Board. It is a further tribute that those good relations stood the strain of what followed.

By June 1932, the economy campaign was in full swing and the W.E.A. received a warning from the Board that it would be necessary to restrict the normal increase in the number of classes. Total grant expenditure for 1930–31 would be taken as a standard and future expenditure would be limited to that figure. This was a bad blow—especially in view of the fact that a number of local education committees were also reducing grant expenditure. It was not until the session 1934–35 that this regime of stabilization was relaxed by the concession of a 7·5 per cent increase in the Board's expenditure, which allowed for a limited expansion of class work by the W.E.A., and later by the Board's concession of resources to allow for a "reasonable expansion" in 1935–36 within the limits of the "total allocations at its disposal". Two years later, renewed discussions with the Board bore fruit in a further revision of grant regulations which involved recognition of two types of university extension work: extension lectures and extension lecture classes, also a new type of course, the university sessional course operated under the joint committees.

It is an ill wind that blows nobody any good. From 1931

onwards events in Europe had been moving towards inter-national anarchy from which emerged the unchecked menacing power of a rearmed and predatory Germany. The reluctant rearmament programme which was Great Britain's only answer to these momentous happenings provided a spurt for the slow recovery which is the normal response of a free-price economy to acute trade depression, and kept the unemployment per-centage at a level which enabled the Unemployment Insurance Fund to pay its debts and concede a slight increase of benefit to a diminishing number of unemployed. There was less talk of national economy and more talk of social welfare, especially after the 1935 General Election, which returned a Conservative Government to power with a diminished majority. In the sphere of education, the Government's declared policy was a return to that of 1931, which involved a progressive attitude in respect of nursery schools, school medical services, adult and technical education and university scholarships. It also involved an undertaking to raise the school-leaving age. But alas! an undertaking comprising a condition which was, in the words of the W.E.A. President, "administratively unworkable and educationally vicious". The school-leaving age was indeed to be raised to fifteen, but local education authorities were to be permitted, at their discretion, to grant exemption to children of fourteen to fifteen years for what was described as "bene-ficial employment". Beneficial to whom? The W.E.A. had its own ideas on the answer to that question which the terms of the Government's Bill left unanswered.

The W.E.A.'s immediate answer was to stiffen its own machinery by establishing an Education Advisory Committee with one of its own vice-presidents, Principal Nicholson of Hull University College, as chairman, and Harold Shearman, by now established as the W.E.A.'s full-time education officer, as secretary.

On the matter of "beneficial employment" the W.E.A. went down fighting. The Education Bill, with this stultifying clause embedded in it, was introduced into the House of Commons on December 19th, 1935, and with this stultifying clause intact, it emerged from the House of Lords on June 17th, 1936. The W.E.A. did its best; but it is to the discredit of the voluntary youth organizations that they played no significant part in this campaign, and the Government might well have persuaded itself that those who cared most for the welfare of young people feared least from this interruption to their education. But fate intervened. The Act, timed to operate as from September 1st, 1939, was caught by the "ill wind" which swept over Europe in that month, blowing into shreds and tatters very much that was good and a little that was bad.

Through these years of political crisis, depression and growing international insecurity, the W.E.A. was carrying a volume of work which continued, with brief intervening periods of stagnation, to expand. Its expansion of staff was, however, in no way proportionate to its expansion of work. In 1927–28 its total salaried staff throughout the country was forty-five, in 1937–38 it was fifty-six. But the number of its branches had increased by one-third. It was, however, better equipped in other respects.

In 1929 a major operation had been done on its constitution in response to complaints that the rank and file of the Association were out of touch with national policy, in fact that as a result of past over-emphasis on local autonomy the W.E.A. had become less a national movement than a number of isolated district movements. The change introduced in 1930, and described by the General Secretary as "a mild revolution" rather than "revision", involved the supercession of the old federal Central Council by a national conference invested with supreme policy-making power, directly representative of the branches, districts and affiliated bodies, and responsible for electing an executive entrusted with governing powers exercised within the framework of national policy between annual meetings of the national conference. The first national conference under the new constitution met at Nottingham in February 1931.

With changes in the constitution went changes in the Central Office. Its location was changed in 1931 owing to the expiry of the lease of 16 Harpur Street. The new office was at 38A St. George's Road, in what was described in the Annual Report of that year as a "quieter neighbourhood" than Bloomsbury. This description is accurate, since St. George's

Road runs through the dreary heart of the vast and featureless peninsula of Pimlico. It is at the same time misleading because the price of such quietness was a remoteness which made the Central Office comparatively difficult of access except by bicycle or private car, and which made it virtually impossible to combine a visit to the office with any other business in the near neighbourhood, with the possible exception of arrival at the continental platform of Victoria Station. The new office required a good deal of reconditioning to make it habitable, but the Carnegie Trust generously contributed £750 towards the cost, and the W.E.A. settled down in company with the Central Joint Advisory Committee and the London District for a long spell of moderate discomfort.

The first General Secretary to preside at number 38A was A. S. Firth, who had succeeded Muir in 1930. For seven years Firth had served as secretary to the Education Department of the Trades Union Congress and was well fitted to maintain close relations with the world of organized labour. But the burden of W.E.A. responsibility was too much for him; his health failed and in 1934, after three months' sick leave, he was advised to transfer to less exacting work. His obvious successor was Ernest Green. Green brought to the work of General Secretary a long experience of W.E.A. activity: first as district secretary in Yorkshire, an office from which he retired on becoming assistant general secretary under Muir. He carried the burden of Central Office work during Muir's long illness, and when Firth succeeded Muir he remained in the Central Office as organizing secretary. But he brought to his new task something more than long experience; he brought an untiring and unshakable devotion—happily combined with physical health to sustain it—which gave stability to its administrative work and continuity to its changing emphasis. He appeared to want nothing for himself other than opportunity to serve his chosen cause; and in later years when rising costs precipitated the question of salary increments it was noticeable that matters were always so arranged by him as to exclude the General Secretary's own meagre salary from discussion.

Two major developments characterized this period of

W.E.A. activity against a turbulent background of internal and external politics. The first was a deliberate attempt to develop educational work in rural areas. This special effort was launched in 1927 with the help of a substantial grant from the Carnegie United Kingdom Trust. For many years a full-time tutor had been operating under the Yorkshire District Council in East Yorkshire. By 1931 seven full-time resident tutors were at work—thanks to both the Carnegie and Cassel Trusts—and considerable progress was reported. In 1933 the Carnegie Trust's grant came to an end, but a reduced grant was given for two more years and the work went forward. The Trusts had, in fact, challenged the W.E.A. to justify its claim that once established, the work would command the support of statutory and university bodies in the areas selected. This, in fact, it did. Of nine resident tutors appointed during the period of grant-aid, five had by 1934 been appointed as staff tutors by the university joint committees in their area. In East Suffolk and the Lindsey Division of Lincolnshire it had not been possible to secure financial resources for staff tutors, but the district organizations in these areas undertook to carry forward the demands arising from pioneer work with the help of their existing panel of tutors. The challenge had been met and the Trusts had reason to know that their money had been well spent.

A second development along similar lines was an attempt to develop non-vocational educational work among young people of eighteen to twenty-five. A proposal put forward by the W.E.A. Executive Committee to the Carnegie Trust for using W.E.A. machinery to broaden the interests of this elusive age-group met with a ready response. In 1936 four full-time youth organizers were appointed for three years to work under *ad hoc* sub-committees appointed by the district councils in their areas. They made it their first business to get into touch with existing local youth organizations for the purpose of supplying from panels of potential lecturers, material of a slightly more educational nature than was otherwise available. On paper their lists of organizations approached and lecturers empanelled was impressive. The extent to which this sporting, dancing, courting age-group profited by the W.E.A.'s effort to educate it will never be known. There was much else to distract it—including compulsory military service—during the continuance of the scheme, which did not survive the Second World War.

Through all these changes and chances there was one W.E.A. activity which achieved a kind of golden age: this was the *Highway*. Since birth it had been handed from one editor to another and much devoted unpaid work had been put into the effort of sustaining it, both by editors and subscribers, but it had never enjoyed continuity of handling. It was, moreover, far more vulnerable than any contemporary organ to seasonal fluctuations. When classes were going strong, class secretaries would act as distributing agents; when classes suspended work the opportunity for such distribution would cease. It was the normal practice of the *Highway* to hibernate during the summer months, but such irregularity of appearance was not conducive to the maintenance of a steady circulation. It was always open to a new editor to try a new approach to his or her elusive clientele, and perhaps to disguise an old approach under a new colour, type, shape, or cover design. There were many new editors and many changes of approach and format, and through these changes the *Highway* continued to rock gently backwards and forwards between the parochial and the academic. During the short reign of Barbara Wootton as editor, between 1923 and 1925, it had appeared as a remarkably well-written academic quarterly. R. S. Lambert, who followed, acted on the assumption that it had become too much of a journal of adult education. It returned to monthly issues. His reign was cut short by his transfer from the service of London University's extra-mural department to that of the B.B.C., where he was presently to emerge as editor of its new organ, *The Listener*. After that D. A. Ross took it over. His handling of it was ambitious but unpredictable. There was, he said, something wrong with a circulation which sticks at about 6,000 while class membership is 30,000. He would try to make it "a student paper". In October 1929, its readers awaited its appearance in vain. Ross had "found it impossible to give attention to the *Highway*". But he bequeathed to his successor a circulation of 8,000. His successor was W. E. Williams and it was then that the *Highway* entered upon its golden age.

For the first time in its history it experienced a decade of editorial continuity. But with W. E. Williams at the helm it experienced a great deal more. It had always been able to command the voluntary services of distinguished writers. Williams's effective contacts even exceeded what had gone before: authoritative names in the sphere of economics, science and literature sparkled from his pages. He gave it special issues on contemporary topics: local government, Russia, Germany, foreign affairs, housing and town-planning, the Co-operative Movement, science, malnutrition. He brought the arts into prominence: films, drama and radio acquired a new significance. In 1934 he revived the practice of issuing district supplements, and thereafter they developed on the grand scale. There was no lack of "news of the movement". From time to time illustrations appeared in it, photographs or cartoons. Partly as a result of these features and partly as a condition which made them possible circulation crept steadily up; in 1931, nearly 11,000; in 1933, 14,000—a record figure; in 1938, 18,500—a new record; in April 1939, 20,000—an even better record. And month by month there appeared editorial notes of so pungent a quality that Williams thought fit to accept personal responsibility by attaching his own name to them. He did not escape criticism and his replies to it were uninhibited; it was the price he paid for the free expression of diverse views. He had it over his German special issue and over his Russian special issue. He had it in 1938 over an article by the Conservative journalist-historian, Arthur Bryant, and his reply was vitriolic. "Are we to give dissentient opinion a hearing", he wrote, "or are we to bawl it out?"—"I stand now where I stood then, in what is rapidly becoming these days the no-man's-land of tolerance and free speech. I stand, first, for the dignity of debate, and second for the principle that, in an educational magazine, we must practise the habit of listening to what must seem to most of us a dissentient opinion." He added: "I have learned by now to look pleasant as I sit in the tumbril. But I am disturbed by this fresh evidence that some responsible elements in our movement are disposed to abandon the traditional attitude of the W.E.A. to controversy." He was right about the attitude of the W.E.A., whose members endorsed his gesture with a rain of appreciative correspondence. But in one respect he deceived himself: he did not look pleasant as he sat in the tumbril, he looked exceedingly displeased—for he had never learned to suffer fools gladly and in the ranks of the W.E.A. there had always been a perceptible minority of fools. How could it have been otherwise with a membership of close on twenty-nine thousand.

Such, indeed, was the strength of the W.E.A. on the eve of World War Number Two. Its finances were, as ever, precarious. From year to year it had shown small deficits and for some of these the *Highway* was responsible, but rigid economies, special donations, and timely help from the Carnegie Trust for administrative expenses kept it from a headlong descent "into the red". It had never ceased its effort of self-criticism and a running inquiry into the "Purpose and Organization of the Association" produced helpful suggestions concerning the assignment of functions to special committees. The years had brought it a new degree of influence in the formation of educational opinion at home, and new stimulating contacts with adult education overseas. They had, as was inevitable, removed some of its most devoted and constructive pioneer workers. Wimble, who had helped to sustain the Central Office in the days of Mansbridge's active leadership and long sick-leave, left in 1923 to organize with distinguished success the Workers' Travel Association. E. J. Hookway, who had served as North-Western District Secretary before the First World War and had served the Central Office before that, departed this life in 1936. A. L. Smith, who had played so large a part in the 1907 university concordat, died in 1924; and Lord Sanderson, who as Sanderson Furniss had presided over the resurrection of Ruskin College in 1919, and guided its destinies thereafter, died in April 1939.

But, perhaps, the most significant break with the past was the death in 1936 of Reuben George, the Grand Old Man of the Swindon W.E.A. Like Mansbridge he had believed with religious passion in "the glory of education" and he would speak of it in language more redolent of William Morris's England than of an England which had learned by experience that human progress towards perfectibility can slip into reverse.

It was, perhaps, a merciful providence that spared him the shame of peace at any price in September 1938, and the horror of total war in September 1939. But the faith which had inspired him, though expressed in very different language, inspired the younger generation that remained to carry on the organization. Once again the W.E.A. had to take the decision that in the event of war, which this time took nobody except the Prime Minister by surprise, the work would go on. It was taken in careful consultation with the Central Joint Advisory Committee and the Board of Education, which agreed that emergency conditions might justify a liberal interpretation of grant regulations. Disturbed class-registration was not, however, the only risk that faced tutors and students as they gathered for the opening of the 1939 session. Knowing something of the latest improvements in military aviation, they had a pretty good idea of what they were in for.

# CHAPTER NINE

# WORLD WAR NUMBER TWO

WHEN World War Number Two materialized at 11 o'clock on September 3rd, everybody knew precisely what to do and where to go. Out from the evacuation areas streamed the children, marshalled by their teachers, bound for their allotted reception areas. Into the vacant schools streamed the civil defence workers. London University softly and silently melted away. Oxford, Cambridge, Bristol, Bangor and Aberystwyth received its component parts. The future of its extra-mural work was obscure. Into its empty lecture and committee rooms streamed the Ministry of Information, the Air Ministry, the B.B.C. and the Tavistock Clinic. Up went the barrage balloons. Down came the black-out. Out came the A.R.P. wardens. And no bombs fell.

The W.E.A. operated with as much precision as was possible under such conditions. The headquarters staff moved from St. George's Road to Holybrook House at Reading, leaving its education officer, Harold Shearman, to hold the fort in London, while the General Secretary swung like a pendulum between the two centres. And the president, R. H. Tawney, composed a message for the first war issue of the *Highway* in which he said, in different but no less arresting words, what Temple had said on a similar occasion in September 1914, namely, that the W.E.A.'s war-time task was to make a contribution to national sanity and that its work would go on. The only difference was that in 1914 there seemed to be some doubt of this intention until it was clarified; in 1939 there was none. A similar decision was taken in connection with the *Highway*. District supplements would have to go. Thirty-two pages would have to come down to twenty-eight, possibly later to twenty. There was, however, paper in hand to see the editor through the session 1940–41, and the *Highway* would continue to appear.

With so many people moving about and with so many of

those who did not move about changing their occupations or undertaking extraneous duties, the prospect of some considerable disorganization of the class programme planned for the session 1939–40 seemed inevitable; especially in London where the supposition that here would be the objective of Germany's first air bombardment had occasioned a curfew order. No grant-aided work was to be undertaken after 6 p.m. within one and a half miles of Leicester Square. Cinemas fared worse: and at Notting Hill Gate a hibernating picture-palace bore a notice to the effect that the nearest show was now at Aberystwyth. But these excessive precautions were of short duration.

Meanwhile all over the country schools where classes had expected to meet were taken over for war purposes or were in some cases found incapable of being effectively blacked-out. It was surprising that any normal programme could be carried through at all under such conditions; but in fact a very large number of normal programmes were. Indeed, when statistics came to be assembled at the end of the session it was found that the decline in the number of grant-earning classes was only 5 per cent, and in the number of students 12·5 per cent. Those which suffered worst were the tutorial classes, whose members or potential members found it difficult to give a firm pledge of three years' continuous work since many of them felt doubtful concerning the probability of three years of continuous existence. The one-year classes operating under the "Further Education" regulations of the local education authorities also suffered badly because the local education authorities' energies were heavily engaged with the import and export of evacuees. Partly because of this contraction of class work, and not, it seems, as a result of increased branch subscriptions imposed in this unfortunate year for the accumulation of a national development fund, there was a reduction in branch and district membership—the first for seven years—as well as in the number of affiliated societies. This last was largely due to the defection of educational bodies, some of which went into cold storage during the war. It was not, happily, due to the defection of trade unions.

But, if normal class work suffered a decline, abnormal class work began almost immediately to make new demands. There were concentrations of civil defence workers to be catered for, balloon barrage units, groups of exiled teachers—and above all, the forces into whose ranks so many potential class members had been absorbed. Army education became a major W.E.A. preoccupation; so, too, did the maintenance of the primary school service under the stress and strain of evacuation. It was, perhaps, regrettable that the first abortive air-raid warnings which followed closely upon the declaration of war had not been accompanied by the dropping of a bomb or two. If they had, the evacuation of children from target areas would have been a more decisive business. As it was—when schools were closed in the evacuation areas, more than half the children remained with their parents. And when, as the winter of 1939 drew to its close, still no bombs fell, evacuees began to trickle back to the danger zones. By Christmas 1939, the trickle had become a stream, but there was no properly organized school life for the children who came back. Compulsory education had virtually ceased to exist. The children were not the only optimists. Londoners who had faced the inconvenience of exile, intensified doubtless by one of the harshest winters within memory, also came back. So did Ernest Green and his staff, "fed-up" with the isolation of Holybrook House from the centre where so much work was now going on, and so much more work was needed.

Then it was that the bombs began to fall—first in London, then later, in the autumn of 1940, in the provinces. The inhabitants of the large towns looked to their air-raid shelters. In many of them the shelters were inhabited, and not without good reason, night after night. If W.E.A. work was to be carried on, into the shelters much of it would have to go, and go it did. Where bombs fell, evening work was an adventure. Where bombs did not fall, thanks to rationed petrol, darkened streets and pin-point headlamps it was, if not adventurous, at least mildly uncomfortable. It is unfortunate for the W.E.A. that the nation's "crisis time" invariably coincides with the period in which class programmes for the coming session are initiated. So it was in the autumn of 1938 when war clouds gathered but did not burst, so it was in the autumn of 1939 when war clouds burst but did not rain bombs. So it was in the autumn of 1940 when the bombs at last began to fall. A national crisis thus occasions the maximum of disturbance to W.E.A. work.

The London District met the situation by concentrating on week-end classes and Saturday afternoon public lectures, its optimism finding expression in an inaugural lecture on "Rebuilding the Capital". But a large proportion of the capital was fated to be unbuilt before the enterprise here contemplated could be actually engaged in.

Under such conditions it is greatly to the credit of those responsible for W.E.A. policy that the membership of the Association, and indeed the volume of its activities, remained intact. It did something more—in 1943 it achieved a new high level. As in the autumn of 1939 so, taking the war period as a whole, it was the tutorial classes which bore the brunt of social upheaval. From 759 classes in 1938–39 they fell to 438 in 1942–43, recovering only to 560 in 1944–45. But grant-earning classes as a whole showed a steady rise during the same period from 3,219 to 4,663, branch and district membership from 28,652 to 40,733, and affiliated societies from 2,199 to 2,612. This war-time achievement may be attributed to two factors: first, the constructive part played by the W.E.A. in educational advance on the legislative front, second, to the flexibility of W.E.A. policy in responding to the educational needs of a war situation. It was the second which led to the multiplication of short-term classes, which drew W.E.A. tutors into unfamiliar places, and confronted them with new types of audience. An outstanding example of such flexibility occurred in the spring of 1942 when a W.E.A. organizer was permitted to advertise his wares at a meeting attended by the inhabitants of a north-country munition workers' hostel. An earlier notice had, it appears, paved his way by the announcement of "W.E.A. Lectures on Health, Beauty, Topical Subjects, Travel, etc." An alternative meeting offered a course on "Beauty and Skin Treatment". The W.E.A. organizer was prepared to compete. Opening his talk with a commentary on the comparative glamour of Joan Bennett, Dorothy Lamour and Greta Garbo, he went on to discuss health in relation to work, work in relation to economics, and so on to world affairs. He seems to have carried his audience with him, for a subsequent subject questionnaire produced fourteen recruits for an economics class, nine for international relations, eleven for colonial history, nineteen for psychology and eight for literature. When one contemplates the large numbers of women who would be resident in one such hostel, anything up to or even exceeding a thousand, such recruitment may seem meagre. When one visualizes the artificiality and excitement of such hostel life, the fact that its members were for the most part wholly unskilled and uneducated, in some cases resentful at being conscripted for industrial work far from home, in others, excited by large earnings unaccompanied by domestic responsibilities, it is easy to realize that W.E.A. tutors and organizers who entered these strange precincts were faced with a tough assignment. What permanent fruit emerged from seeds thus sown we shall never know. So great a faith must, however, generate hope.

A comparable piece of pioneer work was carried through in the construction camps where mobile groups of men were engaged on contract work, often in remote places, usually under harsh conditions. Here, under the joint auspices of the W.E.A. and the Ministry of Labour, Miss Elizabeth Monkhouse set to work in the spring of 1942. Posters preceded the initial meetings. In one camp such advance publicity brought an audience of over two hundred; in another an audience of three. But, unlike the munition workers' hostels, the construction camps contained in many cases a nucleus of skilled men and where this was the case, the going was good. To literature and art the response was cold. To subjects connected with working-class lives and the world situation it was warmer. And everywhere men wanted to learn about Russia—the new ally whose dogged resistance had caused a spectacular diversion of German war potential and brought respite to our bombed cities.

A larger war-time educational venture, however, was the appointment of full-time organizers of classes for civil defence workers. The London District had made a start with A.R.P. workers while they were waiting for bombs to fall in the winter of 1939, and later while bombs were falling in the winter of 1940. But after the cessation of air attacks in the summer of

1941 the work was widely extended, and Merseyside, emerging from a ferocious onslaught of German malice, offered a spectacular response. But response was not confined to these two great centres of war resistance. Up and down the country, the National Fire Service, the Casualty First Aid Stations, Rescue Parties, the Civil Nursing Reserve, the A.R.P. Wardens responded to the offer of classes and discussion groups. So far as could be estimated, some 7,500 of these full-time and part-time civil defence workers were attending short courses during the winter of 1942–43, and former W.E.A. students were playing a significant part as discussion group leaders.

Class attendance can be measured with moderate precision; the fruits of class attendance cannot. When, however, we turn from civil defence to education within the ranks of the serving forces even the measurements of class attendance elude us. We can observe the formation of committees and still more committees, and committees to co-ordinate committees. We can handle documentary proofs of the build-up of a great army education service, and estimate the expansion of personnel assigned to its operation. We can even convince ourselves of the determination and good faith of the higher authorities responsible for its encouragement. But how far such effort reached its mark, how far or how intensively it became part of the serving man's or woman's war-time experience, is more difficult to estimate. Indeed, it is difficult for any such estimate to get much further than a random collection of personal experiences.

The activity of the W.E.A. in respect of army education goes back to the introduction of compulsory military training in May 1939. Clearly the concentration of large numbers of young militia-men in training camps could not go unregarded, and a promising beginning was made after Mr. Creech Jones, who combined membership of Parliament with a vice-presidency of the W.E.A., had moved an amendment to the Military Training Bill imposing upon the Army Council the duty of providing educational facilities for militia-men through statutory and voluntary bodies in consultation with the Board of Education. There followed, thanks to W.E.A. initiative, a consultation between university and other educational bodies and the Board of Education, as a result of which joint adult education committees were set up in each training area to arrange lectures in co-operation with the military authorities. Alas, the outbreak of war brought the militia and its educational programme to an end and the War Office withdrew from the scheme.

When a new beginning was made under war conditions, it was the Y.M.C.A. which took the first effective step by making a grant of £300 towards the cost of army education. Working in co-operation with the W.E.A. a conference was called, the outcome of which was a Central Advisory Committee for Adult Education in H.M. Forces, whose first meeting was held on January 25th, 1940. Very soon twenty-three regional committees were in existence and by the end of the summer, lectures and classes were in full swing with an official undertaking, insisted upon by the W.E.A., that attendance must be voluntary and discussion free. War Office co-operation took the tangible form of substantial grants for the expenses of central and regional administration, and in due course for the appointment of a considerable body of full-time lecturers. The W.E.A. played its part by encouraging its tutors to offer their services and by admitting members of the forces to its classes. In fact, the forces suffered no dearth of lectures. The question for adult education enthusiasts was: can a surfeit of isolated lectures be regarded as education? It was presumably some doubt on this score which prompted the W.E.A. to mobilize the energies of the adult education movement for the provision of forces' correspondence courses. Within a year 7,212 such courses had been taken up and this in spite of an entrance fee of ten shillings. The secretarial work which they involved provided a "spare-time" occupation for Ernest Green at 38A St. George's Road.

But a more systematic effort at army education had meanwhile taken shape. Its moving spirit was W. E. Williams, who for twelve years had edited the *Highway*, and conferred upon it the double blessing of editorial continuity and abundant life. The new venture aimed at bringing general education right into the picture of army training. The War Office itself provided a headquarters Army Bureau of Current Affairs (ABCA to its familiars) from which study outlines in the form of pamphlets went out to service units. It then became the *duty* of the unit officers to set aside periods for the discussion of these pamphlets and actually to lead the discussion themselves. The pamphlets were so arranged as to provide such facts and figures relevant to the subject under discussion as would enable a moderately well-educated serving officer to expound it.

It might at first blush be supposed that informative pamphlets on current affairs compiled and issued under the auspices of the War Office—and issued as confidential documents for fear of provoking contentious public discussion of their contents—would be effective instruments of government propaganda. The fact that the administration of the scheme was handed over to W. E. Williams, who was responsible for the compilation of the pamphlets and the selection of their authors, was an effective guarantee that this would not happen. Only once was there any sign of political pressure on ABCA. In November 1942, there appeared the famous Beveridge Report on Social Insurance. It immediately became a "best seller", the press was full of it; indeed, for a time it held its own with war news in general discussion. Never was there a more vigorously current "Current Affair". ABCA was quick off the mark. The report would inevitably be discussed in every barrack-room—it had better be discussed intelligently. An excellent pamphlet, including a survey by Beveridge himself, went out to army units. It was quickly withdrawn under compulsion of a War Office direction that: "it was thought inappropriate that officially conducted discussions should take place before the Government and Parliament have had an opportunity of considering the report". What took place within the precincts of the War Office between the former editor of the *Highway* and whoever was responsible for this brainless and wholly pointless action remains a mystery. One can, however, surmise that the former editor of the *Highway* did not "look pleasant as he sat in the tumbril", and it is significant that such a thing never happened again. Incidentally, W. E. Williams had by this time become the "former" editor of the *Highway*. War Office duties absorbed all his time and his editorship was handed over to a vice-president of the W.E.A., Mrs. J. L. Stocks, who conducted it through the war period against a tide of rising costs and lengthening printing-time. Indeed, there came a point in 1945 when one month's issue would have to go to press before the preceding month's issue had reached the hands of its readers. Thus its news became stale and its correspondence columns irrelevant. Nevertheless, it survived the Second World War as it had survived the First.

How far this double effort of army education was really effective was—and remains—a matter of some doubt. That the duty of expounding ABCA directives was in many cases never performed is certain. That in many more cases it was performed half-heartedly is also certain. The pages and correspondence columns of the *Highway* during this period contain a running commentary on the deficiencies and achievements of army education and the deficiencies occupy most space. This is only natural. Words always come more readily in response to what one does not like, than in response to what one does like. The vocabulary of denunciation is richer and more imaginative than the vocabulary of praise. In practice, both systems of army education were effective where an officer who happened to have educational interests was ready to hand, and this was by no means everywhere. One civilian observer who had enjoyed a fairly varied contact with military units was heard to refer to army education as "jam tomorrow, jam yesterday, but never jam today". The scheme had been operated—was about to be operated—but for this or that reason it was unfortunately not in operation on the occasion of that particular visitor's advent.

In the field of army education the W.E.A. could boast of a vigorous initiative and a continuing effort. It could not, however, preen itself on having achieved a significant result. In the case of education generally it could, and did. Once again history repeated itself. As in World War Number One, so in World War Number Two, death and destruction, straitened resources and a desperate struggle for material survival brought a new awareness of the importance of education and a new readiness to accept equalitarian standards subversive of the old class pattern. The W.E.A. knew from experience how to take advantage of that "tide in the affairs of men, which taken at the flood, leads on to fortune". And for this it had better machinery than was the case in 1914–18. It had a highly expert Education Advisory Committee, with Harold Shearman as full-time education officer, and Principal Nicholson of Hull University College as chairman. Among its members was Lady Simon, a leading citizen of Manchester, who as chairman of Manchester's Education Committee during the lean years had become a past master in the art of circumventing educational economies, as well as in the practice of going straight to the top levels of the Board of Education and there expounding her views with as much detailed knowledge as was possessed by its senior officers, and a great deal more freedom.

Having been, like Beatrice Webb, a Miss Potter before marriage, it has sometimes been assumed that Lady Simon was a niece of Mrs. Webb. This erroneous assumption is doubtless reinforced by an intellectual affinity; since both these eminent women, separated in time by a generation, command piercing intellectual powers effectively canalized into the particular social reforms they have at heart. Perhaps, too, there is a physical affinity. Female intellect is not invariably reflected in personal beauty. These two Miss Potters were endowed with more than their share of both.

Thus, operating in a sure and certain faith that the paradox of history would repeat itself, the Education Advisory Committee embarked in the first year of the war on the compilation of a blue-print of educational reconstruction.

The first activities, however, had of necessity to be defensive. The chaotic state of elementary education under war conditions and the initial suspension of compulsory school attendance over large areas required attention. In December 1939, a pamphlet by Lady Simon, entitled *The Children in War-Time*, reviewed the situation and made suggestions for its redress. There followed a deputation to the President of the Board of Education led by R. H. Tawney; a week later came an official announcement that compulsory education would be restored in all areas. In due course it was.

Meanwhile, the campaign for fundamental reconstruction went forward and on a wide front. By February 1941, the Co-operative Union, the Trades Union Congress and the W.E.A. were acting together. On February 18th, Creech Jones led a deputation to the Board with the demand for a new Education Bill including the raising of the school-leaving age (without exemptions) as soon as the war should be over. It was sympathetically received by Mr. Ramsbotham, who had succeeded Earl de la Warr as President—but neither Mr. Ramsbotham nor Earl de la Warr were the "Fishers" of whom the educational world was in need. Not till the following July did that "Fisher" appear in the person of R. A. Butler, and the appointment of Butler to an office which ambitious ministers normally avoid suggested that important legislation was in the offing. For R. A. Butler was something more than an ambitious minister. He was outstandingly intelligent and exceedingly energetic; and though he had never cultivated the sub-soil of education and had little experience of its day-to-day working, as a university man of considerable academic distinction he was a denizen of its upper air and respectful of its qualitative standards.

It was about this time that a mysterious little green, paper-covered book began to circulate, entitled *Education after the War*. Mysterious because, issued by the Board of Education, it bore upon its cover the inscription, *Strictly confidential for official use only*, yet anybody in any degree interested seemed to have read it and, indeed, to have acquired a copy. Seldom has a secret document been more publicly discussed. Seldom has an official publication aroused more sanguine expectations. According to its introduction the proposals contained in it were "so framed that the better system of education which they envisage would be equally available to all, irrespective of their means", and on examination these proposals were found to contain nearly all the major reforms which composed the W.E.A.'s reconstruction plan: a school-leaving age of fifteen without exemptions, part-time continued education till eighteen, redefinition of the area of elementary education to allow a transition to secondary education at eleven plus under a single code of regulations covering modern, grammar and technical schools, free secondary education at provided or aided schools, special schools, nursery schools, longer training for teachers, more adequate provision for entrance to universities—all this and more. It was not to be assumed—the introduction made this clear—that these proposals embodied the Board's "considered conclusions". The document was a "basis for discussion" prepared by some officers of the Board, and expressive of their "personal views". But the fact that such views found expression in a document whose confidential contents had been permitted and, indeed, encouraged to leak out in all directions was significant. Clearly it was for this that Butler had been sent to the Board of Education.

If the "green book" was in the nature of a finger on the pulse of public opinion it was the W.E.A.'s business to see that the pulse had a firm beat. The Bill embodying constructive reform might be delayed—this must be prevented. What did the Government propose to do with these existing citadels of class privilege: the "public schools"? There had been no indication. Nor was it clear that the "dual system" with its acceptance of defective standards and tardy reform in non-provided schools would be brought to an end. When Mr. Butler's Bill appeared it might be too timid—it probably would be. Indeed, it might never appear.

By the summer of 1942 the W.E.A.'s blue-print of an equalitarian system of national education had behind it a powerful quadruple alliance in the shape of a Council for Educational Advance, comprising the W.E.A., the Co-operative Union, the Trades Union Congress, and the National Union of Teachers. J. J. Mallon was its chairman, Harold Shearman its honorary secretary, and Ernest Green its honorary treasurer. It took the field in time to welcome and criticize the Government's White Paper on Educational Reconstruction, whose proposals, though not completely adequate, were better than might have been expected. Thus began the campaign of conferences, public meetings, deputations, publications—reminiscent of the 1917–18 agitation but with a larger force of organized opinion behind it and riper experience to direct it—which led up to the passage of the Butler Education Act on August 3rd, 1944.

All this had meant a high concentration of W.E.A. energy: so much so as to provoke expressions of rank and file discontent at the W.E.A. Annual Conference in October 1943. Were the National Officers and Central Executive so obsessed with the progress of the Education Bill, that insufficient attention was devoted to the advance of adult education which was, after all, the primary concern of the W.E.A.? It was only in return for a solemn promise to take note of the disquiet and endeavour to redress the balance that delegates were prepared to pass the emergency resolution on the Government's White Paper, submitted by the executive committee.

There can be little doubt, however, that the W.E.A. was adopting a far-sighted policy in pursuit of its own larger aims when it threw its weight into the campaign for educational advance during the difficult passage of Mr. Butler's Bill— difficult not because any articulate section of public opinion was ranged against the principle of equalitarian education— the time had gone by when anyone would dare to do that. It was difficult because the age-long curse of English education was still potent. There were some who would have preferred no Bill to a Bill which they considered prejudicial to their own sectarian interests. Mr. Butler had a hard job with them and the W.E.A. regretted the extent of his eventual compromise with the dual system. Nevertheless, it was a great measure and in its far-reaching effects a potentially revolutionary measure. The class-structure in which the W.E.A. had its roots had been held in place by a system of education which perpetuated and intensified economic inequalities by confining the best paid and most responsible jobs to those whose parents were sufficiently well-off to buy the necessary education and training. The Butler Act provided the framework of a system which slowly or rapidly, according to the quality of its subsequent administration, was calculated to iron out those inequalities of opportunity, and thus of income and of power. Such inequalities might still perpetuate themselves through one or more generations, but the state system of education no longer offered them safe conduct; on the contrary it menaced their operative causes. Yet an all-party Government sponsored the 1944 Act, and a Conservative minister was its pilot. By such paradoxical occurrences parliamentary democracy renews its strength.

In fact, the campaign for educational advance did not appear to sap W.E.A. activities in other directions, though as we have seen, many of those other directions, thanks to war needs and war frustrations, led it into unfamiliar paths. Its annual conferences, after preliminary disturbance, renewed their tempo. After a judicious suspension of large assemblies during the "phoney war" period of 1939–40, a national annual conference was planned in Leeds for November 1940, and the Central Office got as far as a preliminary agenda. But the response from branches was poor and bombs had by now begun to fall, so the conference was called off and instead three regional conferences were planned for the following spring in Bangor, Oxford and Leeds, at all of which attention was directed to "Planning the New Education Order".

By the summer of 1942 the German armies were directing their malice eastward and bombs on Great Britain were few and far between. The W.E.A., therefore, assembled for its national annual conference in what the German air force had left of Toynbee Hall. Educational reconstruction was by this time well under way: there were large matters of policy to be discussed, and one major event to applaud: William Temple, its ex-president, had been appointed Archbishop of Canterbury. The conference had, however, to do without its president-regnant, R. H. Tawney, who had been sent to Washington as the first labour attaché to the British Embassy. Harold Clay presided in his stead as acting president. In the following year the conference met again at Toynbee Hall, this time with R. H. Tawney back in the presidential chair. Only once more was he destined to occupy it—at the last war-time annual conference of the W.E.A., in January 1945, in Caxton Hall, Westminster. This time the German armies were in retreat, but their final parting shots were aimed at London, and delegates from the provinces had an opportunity of hearing, in the intervals of debate, the muffled roll of thunder and the double explosion of a V 2 rocket.

It was a significant occasion, this last conference of the second war period; not only because it granted R. H. Tawney release from the presidency for which he had been agitating with increasing urgency after sixteen years of strenuous leadership. Harold Clay took his place, but further reference to him belongs to the post-war period. The Caxton Hall conference was also important because though fighting was still in progress and rockets still flying, it was clearly a post-war discussion and the post-war conduct of the W.E.A. was, in its various aspects, the main content of the agenda. At one point high policy occasioned an outbreak of acute controversy. In spite of the war W.E.A. activities had expanded enormously. W.E.A. financial resources had not. Grants of public money seemed easy to come by. Should not application be made for such assistance towards W.E.A. administrative costs? For years grants had been accepted in aid of salaries for teachers and organizers, and this without compromising freedom of discussion—it was but a short step and an urgently needed step to ask for something more. Successive speakers expounded its indubitable expediency. R. H. Tawney was the last speaker. Briefly, but decisively, he outlined the case for independence as opposed to affluence. The W.E.A., he admitted, faced the future with a heavy burden of administrative work. Should that burden be lightened "at the cost of undermining the spiritual independence of the movement"? The W.E.A. resolved its doubt. Its answer was: No.

One other memory shadows this last war-time national conference. The loss of a president caused regret, but R. H. Tawney was still there, his counsel would be available to the Association, his speeches would enliven its meetings, his personality would be part of its abundant life. The loss of its ex-president occasioned regret of a different order. Here was high tragedy. As delegates stood in silence remembering the death on October 26th, 1944, of William Temple, many of them must have realized the magnitude of something more than the Association's loss. An Archbishop of Canterbury who in scarcely more than two years had conjured up the vision of a Christian Church speaking wisdom to a responsive people, had passed from the scene—and with his passing the vision faded.

So the W.E.A. faced the future having chosen the harder financial way. War-time experience had not mitigated its hardness. The ratio of assumed obligations to administrative resources continued to shift against the administrative resources. Other things moved too: railway fares, printing and paper costs. If they did not eat up more of the Association's spendable income it was because of drastic economies and a monstrous curtailment of salaries. Because of these, the first war year left a balance of £173 17s. 10d. on revenue and expenditure account. The second war year left a balance of £100. Economies had more than kept pace with the decline of branch contributions. The third war year left a balance of £20. The fourth, a balance of £9. There were no more balances after that. On the contrary, in the last war year there was a deficit of £95— but this was due to one large item of expenditure: the printing of a series of reports on post-war policy compiled by the *ad hoc* committee on organization which was reconstituted for this purpose in March 1933. On the other hand, a substantial national development fund amounting in 1945 to £3,111 specially contributed to enable the National Association to give timely help to its districts, was an element of strength to the Association as a whole, and an indication that initiative in the districts would not wither and perish for want of initial encouragement.

In another direction, too, thought was given to the Association's internal contacts. In the last year of the war there was a new overhaul of its constitution. Looking back through the years of its long history, it would almost seem as though the W.E.A.'s major failure has been a failure to get its constitution right. Like an awkward customer in a tailor's shop it never succeeds in feeling comfortable in its clothes. As with clothes, so with constitutions, external fashions change and design must respond to them. Moreover, the customer may protest that his own figure changes: here and there bulges develop and for comfort's sake they must be accommodated. Let us, then, admit that the customer is always right and that the W.E.A.'s constitutional contortions are the result of a right and proper response to external and internal developments rather than to any suspicion of inept constitution-making. At any rate, as the war drew to its close and the Association's work and membership so creditably expanded, it seemed clear that the Central Executive Committee elected by the National Conference, gave insufficient representation and, indeed, insufficient continuous responsibility to districts and affiliated societies. A Central Council was therefore established, composed of representatives of districts and national affiliated bodies, with the addition of eight co-opted members. To it was transferred the duty of appointing an executive committee for the conduct of day-to-day business. The new Central Council met for the first time in July 1945, and thereafter it continued to meet quarterly on a Saturday morning in London, in some place other than the Central Office, which had no room capable of housing so large an assembly.

It was a common complaint among academic personnel during these six years of war that German occupation of the continent and the peril of the seas had cut them off from normal contacts resulting from foreign travel and induced in them a feeling of insular claustrophobia. W.E.A. personnel did not fare so badly in this respect. From the early days of Mansbridge's mission to the self-governing dominions the Association had cultivated its overseas contacts; Ernest Green in particular had always regarded adult education across the seas as a field from which to draw and to which to give encouragement and information. In the summer of 1943 he and two W.E.A. tutors, R. H. Jones and J. Parker, accepted an invitation from the American Workers' Education Bureau to lecture throughout the length and breadth of the United States. In the following year Harold Shearman, Elizabeth Monkhouse and the South-Yorkshire district secretary, E. Fisher, followed in their footsteps.

Meanwhile, at home, there were new adjustments to be made in a field which was becoming increasingly populated by organizations interested in adult education and desirous of talking about it. Years earlier Mansbridge had founded a British Institute of Adult Education. It was in the nature of a learned society, with pleasant London headquarters in Blooms-bury, and under the beneficent presidency of Lord Haldane it aimed at the promotion of research and at the encouragement of experiment. It had a limited individual membership, and with the help of the Cassel Trust promoted a succession of interesting conferences. During the Second World War it became apparent to some people that there were enough voluntary and statutory bodies engaged in adult education to justify some further attempt to co-ordinate and define the sphere of their activities. William Temple and Sir Richard

Livingstone, President of Corpus Christi College, Oxford, were particularly concerned in the matter. Could the British Institute of Adult Education undertake the job? Its constitution and somewhat intensive field of activity hardly suggested that it could. It was, after all, primarily a research body and desired to remain so. There ensued a succession of conferences at which representatives of interested bodies discussed adult education at great length, up and down and round about, the final outcome of which was a National Foundation for Adult Education. This proved to be an ephemeral body. Three years after its establishment in 1946, it amalgamated with the British Institute to become the National Institute of Adult Education for England and Wales. As a consultative and conference-promoting body the National Institute embarked upon an active existence, with an office in Marylebone and a full-time secretary. The W.E.A.—which played an active part in the birth of the Foundation—has since become an affiliate of the Institute.

Looking back at the six years of World War Number Two, it is probably true to say that from a welter of destruction and disruption education emerged triumphant—education in general and, with the exception of the tutorial classes, adult education in particular. Larger powers, more effective machinery, and expanded national resources were within its grasp. So much the more formidable were the problems ahead of those in charge of it—of education in general and of the W.E.A. in particular. But with the close of the war period a number of its leading personalities withdrew from active office and new men stepped into their places. In January 1945, George Thompson, who with an interval of six years in New Zealand had served as district secretary in Yorkshire since 1914, retired. He was the most invincible of fighters in the cause of working-class education and the vitality of Yorkshire's educational life was part of his vitality—as Leeds University recognized when it made him an honorary M.A. In the summer of the same year Mrs. Silyn Roberts retired from the district secretaryship of North Wales, and Eli Bibby from that of the North-Western District. Bibby had carried the burden of its work since 1919, through the hopes of the 'twenties, the depression of the 'thirties and the disruption of the 'forties. E. S. Cartwright, veteran of the pioneer Longton class, retired from the secretaryship of the Oxford Tutorial Classes Joint Committee after thirty-three years of service, the flame of enthusiasm, which always seemed to kindle in him a peculiar grace, burning as brightly as ever. And T. W. Price, veteran of the pioneer Rochdale class, who had served the W.E.A. in almost every sphere it had to offer since the years of its infancy, made his final exit from a life of effort and achievement.

New men, a new president, a new Government, a new Minister of Education, new horizons as the German war potential rolled back from the Continent of Europe leaving distress and disorganization in its wake—and a new address for the W.E.A.'s Central Office; since the London County Council, with the tidy intention of eliminating duplication of street names, had rechristened St. George's Road, St. George's Drive. But it was the same old office, only with a lot more work to do in the same old backwater of Pimlico.

# CHAPTER TEN

# THE POST-WAR YEARS

THE most significant feature of the years which followed the Second World War was a profound modification of the British class-structure by a series of developments comparable in their social and ideological effects to the industrial revolution of a century and a half earlier. Like that earlier revolution the developments were not catastrophic. Unlike that earlier revolution they precipitated no constitutional upheaval; indeed, in so far as they involved legislative action they were carried out within the framework of the British Constitution as completed by the Parliament Act of 1912 and the Franchise Act of 1928. But like the earlier industrial revolution the operative causes of change lay far, but not quite so far back in history. The Liberal administration of 1905–14 explored the possibility of progressive taxation assisted by a supertax. Two subsequent wars taught chancellors of the exchequer what the tax-payer could be persuaded to tolerate in the way of redistributive taxation. That same Liberal administration laid the foundations of a system of national insurance of which inter-war governments made fumbling but, on the whole, expansive use. The acceptance of the social philosophy of a "Welfare State" as expounded in the Beveridge Report, a semi-official document published in 1942, enabled an all-party war-time government to progress on lines which in many respects challenged the basic assumptions of a free-price economy. The war-time experience of rationing and state control of productive processes had already familiarized the public with the idea that the possession of purchasing power does not necessarily confer the right to buy in a free market or direct the flow of capital investment. The advent of a Labour Government, with, for the first time in history, an effective majority, enabled the principles of the Welfare State to be further elaborated. War-time taxation and controls were retained and operated as the instruments of a planned economy designed to eliminate the causes of mass destitution, equalize purchasing power, and ensure for all, the material bases of health, education and reasonable standards of material comfort.

If future commentators rely upon the daily press or upon contemporary novelists for their impressions of these post-war years, they will acquire a picture of unprecedented material austerity. In fact, with the admittedly important exception of housing, the great mass of the population enjoyed better food, better clothes, better health, more varied and lavish entertainment, great mobility, and more leisure than ever before. It was the professional class and the country gentry that bore the brunt of the change—and both were highly articulate. The overwhelmingly larger lower income groups benefited. Meanwhile, a relatively small property-owning group appeared, to judge from its level of expenditure, to have eluded the rigours of combined income and sur-tax rising to 19s. 6d. in £1. Untaxed expense allowances and capital appreciation doubtless explained much of this spectacular phenomenon —doubtless also a readiness to use inherited capital for current consumption which would have shocked our nineteenth-century forebears who feared neither runaway inflation nor confiscatory legislation. It must, however, be admitted that the successful maintenance of boom conditions during five years or so of post-war dislocation owed something to the existence of a seller's market for British exports and something to financial assistance from the U.S.A.—conditions offering scarcely less guarantee of permanence than the continuance in office of a government whose policy was geared to the conception of a planned economy.

Meanwhile, to the social changes resulting from a redistribution of purchasing power and the operation of government controls were added social changes resulting from modification, slower and less spectacular, in the structure of industry. Thanks to the advance of mechanization, the growth of the clerical grades, and the expansion of occupations catering for administration and leisure-time activities, the proportion of "black-coated" to horny-handed manual workers increased. This, added to the decline of domestic service due to heavy taxation on the one side and full employment on the other,

helped to blur the old class pattern which had conditioned the
early life and activities of Albert Mansbridge. It could still be
discerned—but here and there its outlines were fading—had,
indeed, faded. Society was in process of transition, and it was a
transition more rapid and more readily perceptible to those
who lived through it, than the transition which had changed
the mercantile agrarian economy of 1750 into the industrial
free-price economy of 1850.

It is difficult for individuals to adapt themselves to changed
conditions in a changing world. It is more difficult for organizations with their constitutional machinery, their policy statements, their overlapping generations of devotees, and in all
probability their longer history. But it was precisely such an
effort of adaptation that was demanded of the W.E.A. in the
years following 1945.

As the Second World War had cast long shadows before, so
its ending took nobody by surprise. Like most other organizations, like the Government itself, the W.E.A. had planned for
peace long before peace actually came. The W.E.A. and
universities, the W.E.A. and local education authorities,
the W.E.A. and the working-class movement, the relation
between districts and centre, the W.E.A. and large towns, the
W.E.A. and rural areas, the W.E.A. and young workers, the
W.E.A. and institutional and residential adult education—all
these matters and the problems they were likely to raise in the
post-war era had been the subject of reports presented to the
last war-time annual conference and all had been the subject
of discussion. One matter, however, was not a subject of
discussion: the choice of the man who was to succeed R. H.
Tawney as president. That required no discussion. Harold Clay
was so obviously the right man.

That he was a chairman of genius, his colleagues had reason
to know, since as vice-president he had in the past deputized
for R. H. Tawney; had in fact carried the office of acting
president during Tawney's war-time absence in the U.S.A.
No turbulence ruffled him, no tangle of procedure muddled
him. No obstructiveness prevented him from forging ahead
with the business of a meeting. "I contend, Mr. President,
this action is unconstitutional." Some will remember this

protest from the floor. "I agree", was the quiet reply from the chair, "but it's the way we're going to act." There was no further protest, nor was the reply an act of dictatorship, merely the acceptance of a reasonable elasticity for the purpose of enabling the meeting to achieve a result which was generally desired.

But proficiency in the technique of chairmanship was not the only reason for the unanimous choice of Harold Clay as president. In choosing him, the W.E.A. emphasized its determination to go forward into the post-war era closely linked, even more closely linked, with the working-class organizations whose educational expression the Association was designed to be. At the time of his election, Harold Clay was assistant general secretary to the Transport and General Workers' Union, a member of the Labour Party's Executive Committee and chairman of its Advisory Committee on Education. His university had been a Leeds tutorial class; his adopted homeland was the West Riding of Yorkshire, and he spoke with its accents. His whole working life had been bound up with the development of his union and the progress of the W.E.A.; he saw the two as a common cause, and as a common cause he had served them as tutor, negotiator, organizer, administrator.

The new president soon found himself equipped with new officers. Harold Shearman, who for ten years had played a leading part as education officer in the campaign for the 1944 Butler Education Act, was appointed in 1946 as Academic Adviser to the London University Tutorial Classes Committee. This new job gave him an influential position in the sphere of adult education, as well as a more commodious office in a more accessible neighbourhood. But as a vice-president of the W.E.A. his advice and experience remained at its disposal. He was succeeded by Edmund Poole, a young man who had risen from the ranks of the W.E.A. and graduated at Cambridge University. Meanwhile, on the trade-union side the staff was strengthened by the appointment of Harry Nutt as organizing secretary. He combined trade-union experience with experience of W.E.A. work as former district secretary in the East Midlands, and had, like Mansbridge, begun his career as a co-operative employee. And in the last year of the war a new honorary office had been created, that of deputy president, to which Mrs. J. L. Stocks, sometime tutor in the North-Western District and war-time editor of the *Highway*, was elected. For the rest, Ernest Green as General Secretary provided continuity, J. J. Mallon as honorary treasurer provided gaiety.

The first post-war conference was held in November 1945 at Blackpool and its agenda reflected the expansive exuberance of that effulgent resort. The W.E.A. appeared to be contemplating a world hungry for adult education and the Association had an interest in every conceivable educational pie. The Annual Report for that year summed up its mood when it surmised that "the Association stands on the threshold of greater opportunities for the expansion of its work than ever before". There were indeed encouraging features in the situation quite apart from the fact that lights were once more shining from unshrouded windows and the killing had stopped. The 1945 General Election had placed a Government firmly in power whose composition foreshadowed educational enthusiasm in high places. A W.E.A. vice-president, Creech Jones, was Under-Secretary for the Colonies. Fourteen members of the Government, including the Chancellor of the Exchequer, were tutors, former tutors, or members of the W.E.A. Executive. Fifty-six active W.E.A. adherents, tutors or students as the case might be, were Members of Parliament. With Ellen Wilkinson at the Ministry (no longer the misnamed Board) of Education it looked as though the administration of the Butler Act would be bold and resolute. And a new set of grant regulations for adult education flashed an encouraging green light beside the way ahead of voluntary bodies and university extra-mural departments. The word was "Go"—and it was Butler who gave it, before his departure from the Board which he had transformed into a Ministry. The new regulations expressed official confidence in voluntary bodies and universities undertaking "the liberal education of persons of at least 18 years of age", by removing conditions in regard to class attendance, by relating the grant to the total programme of the voluntary providing body and by facilitating the appointment of full-time organizing tutors. In practice, the principal, if not the only, voluntary body operating these regulations on a significant scale was the W.E.A. They were cut to its pattern.

Butler initiated the new grant regulations, it was left to Ellen Wilkinson to promulgate them. Much else was left to her. The 1944 Act had to be brought into operation, a task which in her first year of office involved the issue of some sixty circulars to local authorities and the publication of over eighty administrative memoranda—the majority of which introduced important changes. The outstanding problem, however, was the operation of the clause relating to the school-leaving age. The Act required that it be raised to fifteen as from April 1st, 1945, subject to the Minister's power to postpone this date for not more than two years should the lack of buildings and teachers make this necessary. In fact it did. In fact it always would. There was, in consequence, considerable pressure on the Minister to concede further postponement, and this was accentuated by the state of the labour market which could, it was contested, ill spare the labour force of the 14–15 age-group. Ellen Wilkinson did not yield. The answer of the Ministry was to press on with a system of emergency teacher training colleges, and hope for the best. They were encouraged by a deputation organized by the Council for Educational Advance and led by R. H. Tawney, which waited upon the Minister on December 19th, 1945, to press for more rapid progress with the emergency colleges and the raising of the school-leaving age to sixteen as soon as possible.

There was, indeed, a large task of propaganda ahead of the W.E.A. and the bodies working in association with it for educational advance, for of what use to show a green light if there is insufficient motive power to get the traffic moving? A provision of the Butler Act required local education authorities to survey their areas and submit development plans for all grades of education, primary, secondary and "further". The Act certainly strengthened the power of the Ministry, but much still depended upon the enthusiasm and efficiency with which local authorities operated the new system. Much, in turn, depended on the vigilance and political judgment of the W.E.A.'s Education Advisory Committee. The retirement of Principal Nicholson from its chairmanship in 1946 was happily compensated by the appointment of Lady Simon as his successor. Expert guidance was thus assured.

There were other encouraging signs about this new era of peace and progress. Tutorial classes showed a small but significant expansion. Clearly the war-time ebb-tide had turned. Northern Ireland moved into the picture as a budding W.E.A. district. An earlier attempt to extend W.E.A. activities to Southern Ireland had unhappily broken on the question of textbooks. Like the Central Labour College, Southern Irish educators insisted on their own orthodoxy. But further afield the gospel of adult education was consolidating its forces. In October 1945, to the delight of Ernest Green, who regarded the world as his parish, the International Federation of Workers' Educational Associations came into being, with the W.E.A. as convening body. Its advent foreshadowed a succession of international summer schools and much profitable interchange of students.

Another venture which reflected the optimism of 1945 was the initiation of a project for developing residential courses for adult students. It was no new idea; indeed, it was no new practice; but a belief that there existed an increased potential demand for this more intensified form of adult education was widely shared. It was shared by a number of local education authorities as well as more than one university, and the evacuation of "stately homes" by the heavily taxed and domestically untended owners seemed to offer new possibilities of acquiring these residences for socially useful purposes.

It was the generosity of Sir Richard Acland which opened up a prospect of such residential adult education to the W.E.A. Generations of Aclands had served the cause of education in their own county of Devon and on the national front, and the W.E.A. was delighted to be the recipient of the Acland family home, "Sprydon," at Broadclyst, in North Devon. It was a delightful house which would with a certain amount of alteration make an attractive centre for groups of adult students, twenty-four at a time, engaged in short residential courses, subsidized, it was hoped, by scholarships provided by trade unions and other educationally minded bodies. The terms of the gift were exceedingly generous on Sir Richard Acland's part, and the W.E.A. announced that "Sprydon" would be ready to open as a residential centre in the summer of 1947. But a lot of work would have to be done before that, in the way of publicity, quite apart from the business of internal reconstruction, staffing and furnishing.

There was quite a lot of work, too, to be done on the problem of W.E.A. finance. If the W.E.A. was to escape the odium of becoming a sweating-shop, salaries had to be brought into some relation with scales prevailing in circles less disposed to give devoted labour for less than its market price. A deficit of £752 on the first post-war year's working was a bad basis for the expansion contemplated in all directions. All over the country the W.E.A. was in need of suitable premises where classes could be held and where some kind of social common-room life could be generated. And the headquarters premises in Pimlico were really past bearing. There was scarcely room to move in them, quite apart from the difficulty visitors would normally experience in locating them. There must be a dignified and commodious headquarters, and it was agreed with acclamation that such headquarters must bear the honoured name of the Association's first president: William Temple. With these ends in view it was decided to launch a national appeal for a £100,000 Endowment Fund. It had strong support. Among the names of those who invited contributions were Ernest Bevin, Margaret Bondfield, A. V. Alexander, Arthur Greenwood and William Beveridge; and from the world of education, Walter Moberly, Eustace Percy and Lester Smith, to mention only a few selected at random. And it started well. The first post-war year produced nearly a quarter of the sum aimed at. All things considered, it may be said that the close of the first year of peace found the W.E.A.'s barometer at "set fair".

The second post-war year had scarcely begun when there were signs that another barometer was moving in the opposite direction. With the winter of 1946 came the worst weather within living memory. Snow fell and froze and thawed and froze again on the top of the thaw. Fuel supplies ran short, here and there gas failed and electricity was curtailed. Students and tutors had to face nightly discomforts which recalled the rigours of bombs and black-out minus the war-time zest. It was small wonder that the Annual Report for the year 1946–47 indicated "obstacles" in contrast to the "high hopes" of the preceding year. There were others. The progress of the residential college at "Sprydon" was held up by the realization that a water supply which had been sufficient for the Acland family was insufficient for twenty-four adult students plus staff. Boring operations had to be undertaken to find an alternative source; in the end it was found, but the business took time. And the untimely death of Ellen Wilkinson cast a shadow; but the fact that her successor, George Tomlinson, was an ex-W.E.A. student with all the right ideas, meant no loss of confidence in ministerial intentions; only in ministerial possibilities, for the nation's finance was moving towards a crisis and a new government economy campaign cast its shadow before. Meanwhile, the W.E.A.'s own financial position was deteriorating rapidly. The year 1946–47 shows a deficit on revenue and expenditure account of £2,754. Finance was bound to be a major preoccupation of the third post-war year.

The situation was saved by the trade unions and the trade unions got as good as they gave. It is somewhat difficult not to be convinced by those experimenters with time who see the time-process as a spiral in which patterns of events are superimposed upon similar patterns of an earlier date, rather than as a ticker-tape strip passing in a continuous stream from machine to waste-paper basket. There was certainly in this new post-war era a significant repetition of the pattern of W.E.A. history as it had developed after the First World War. Under pressure of external events in the educational world, and a multitude of new challenging interests, the W.E.A. had to look upon itself and consider whether its primary function— the educational service of organized labour—was receiving adequate attention. The machinery of the Workers' Educational Trade Union Committee, whose formation had been the response to that same question in the 'twenties, was still there. Meanwhile, the need for thoughtful and well-informed labour leadership was urgent as never before. It was not merely that organized labour now held the reigns of government and was a mighty force in Parliament. It was that organized labour was faced with a number of significant changes in the structure of industry which demanded acute analytical comprehension. The conservatism of a trade unionist in regard to his own status and function can be as tenaciously resistant as that of a retired cavalry officer discussing a tank offensive in terms of the charge of the Seventeenth Lancers at Omdurman. The operation of full employment in a semi-planned and partially nationalized economy presented problems very different from those inherent in the situation described by Mr. and Mrs. Webb in *Industrial Democracy* under the chapter heading "Higgling of the Market", where the function of the trade union is related to a quadruple process of unfettered competition characteristic of the eighteen-nineties. It was necessary that these changes together with their political and economic implications should be recognized and understood.

It was certainly recognized by those who attended the first post-war W.E.A. annual conference that an educational campaign directed to the rank and file of the trade-union movement must be vigorously pressed forward. It was also recognized that although the membership of a university tutorial class was the royal road to understanding, great efforts must be made to meet the needs of those unlikely to respond immediately to such austere educational demands. With this aim, the unions affiliated to the W.E.T.U.C. doubled their financial allocations to the central W.E.T.U.C., on the understanding that half the fund so contributed should be spent on pioneer educational activities. That this policy found its mark was shown by the ready response of trade-union members to the offer of one-day and week-end schools which, during 1947–48, reached record proportions. There were even more solid results. In that year, the first of a series of residential courses for members of particular unions was organized, and the Amalgamated Union of Foundry Workers produced a group of selected students for a summer school on the work of that particular union and of unions in general in a changing society. A year later, the National Union of Agricultural Workers followed suit with a group of a hundred selected students, and the Railway Clerks' Association with fifty. The Foundry Workers repeated their effort with a group of thirty members. And that was only a beginning.

The year 1947–48 was, however, notable not merely for the expansion of W.E.T.U.C. activities in its own field. It was the year in which the trade-union movement brought financial salvation to the W.E.A. as a whole. An appeal to affiliated unions to contribute on a *per capita* basis to central funds produced an additional revenue of £4,119. This, added to the proceeds of a B.B.C. appeal by Lord Lindsay, an increase of branch membership subscriptions and the ready response to a district levy, resulted in a balance on income and expenditure account of £1,699. It was noted that another such year would cancel the 1946–47 deficit. In fact it did.

With the wolf in retreat from the door energies were freed for concentration on the job of educational service in return for financial support. A proposal initiated from within the trade-union movement itself that the Trades Union Congress should centralize educational work through the operation of a fund administered by its own Education Committee was duly considered by that body, but finally rejected on the ground that existing organizations were meeting the need. It remained, therefore, to perfect the machinery of the W.E.T.U.C. and bring it into closer relationship at district level with the work of the W.E.A. This was done in 1949, on the recommendation of a sub-committee appointed by the W.E.T.U.C. in 1947. The new constitution provided that the W.E.T.U.C. should operate only at national level, the work of its former divisional committees being transferred to trade-union advisory committees in each W.E.A. district. These committees were to consist of representatives of all such unions in the area as were concerned with W.E.A. educational schemes, and were in their turn to be represented on the district executives. From a central fund built up on a *per capita* contribution of ½d. per union member, money was to be ear-marked for the appointment by the W.E.A. of organizers entrusted with the work of stimulating educational interests among trade unionists. To this new machinery there appeared to be a satisfying response—from the W.E.A. district organizations on the one hand, from the locally represented unions on the other. It remains, however, for the historian of the W.E.A.'s centenary celebrations to chronicle its long-term efficacy.

Meanwhile, ebb and flow in W.E.A. finance kept pace with flow and ebb in the national economy. The requirements of a prodigious defence programme and the cessation of Marshall Aid from the U.S.A. caused history to repeat itself in yet another respect. The precariously balanced Labour Government which emerged from the General Election of 1949 (by the usual ill-starred fate its upheaval coincided with the crucial period of W.E.A. class enrolment) had to meet pressing demands for economy. In the sphere of education the new Government foreshadowed "some slowing down of our advance". The nature of the "slowing down" was explained in circulars 209 and 210. The Education Advisory Committee mobilized its quadruple alliance and prepared its detailed response. But worse was to come. With the advent of a Conservative Government in the following autumn, Great Britain acquired a Prime Minister second to none in his mastery of the English language and his knowledge of its political institutions. But education was not among his major interests and a random guess might suggest that he would be prepared, with very little compunction, to regard it as a suitable field for retrenchment. Nor was misgiving allayed by his appointment of Miss Florence Horsbrugh as Minister for Education. Miss Horsbrugh was known to be an experienced and competent administrator in other fields. The precise temperature of her passion for educational advance was not known. There was, however, some comfort in the presence of R. A. Butler at the Exchequer. The W.E.A. knew all about him, and it was fortunate that university grants depended on the Treasury's generosity to the University Grants Committee rather than that of the Ministry of Education. But his task as paymaster of the universities was comparatively easy. A little money goes a long way when applied to higher education or, for that matter, to adult education. But a lot of money goes a short way when applied to the vast complex of primary and secondary education, and it was, of course, the duty of Miss Horsbrugh to economize. The question was, would the duty be accepted with the pained reluctance of a victim who has been handed a knife with instructions to amputate his own toes, or would it be accepted willingly as one accepts honourable participation in a socially desirable enterprise? It was the business of the Education Advisory Committee to ensure that the response of the Ministry to government pressure was as reluctant as possible and that the response of local education authorities to ministerial pressure was more reluctant still. For this enterprise it had, thanks to the earlier achievements of the W.E.A., no less than 150 local correspondents, members of the Association serving on local education committees up and down the country, strategically placed for conveying information to headquarters on the local operation of educational economies, as well as for reflecting in local administration the policy of educational advance. The outcome of this campaign will provide a further chapter for the W.E.A.'s centenary historian.

One relatively small reflection of the Association's descent to solid earth from the starlit altitude of 1945 deserves a place in its story, since it is the business of an honest historian to record failure as well as achievement. The launching of a workers' residential college at "Sprydon" was undertaken with high hope in 1945. The installation of an adequate water supply delayed but did not quench the expectation of its realization. There were other delays connected with structural alterations; but the hope remained alive, only instead of 1947 the opening was to be in 1950. It was only when its furnishing was completed and a selection committee at work on the appointment of a principal that a decision was taken to postpone opening until the spring of 1951, by which time the hope had died a lingering death. In fact, there appeared to be no enthusiastic demand for more residential courses. Maybe the drive for production in the defence industries afforded too little leisure for residential education. Maybe the hope had been something of an illusion from the start. When 1951 came "Sprydon" was diverted to other, but no less worthy uses, and the W.E.A. was lucky to retrieve its miscalculation without substantial loss. The generosity of Sir Richard Acland's gift in 1945 was equalled by the generosity of his sympathetic understanding when, in 1951, he was told of the W.E.A.'s failure to make use of it.

In another direction, however, hope was triumphantly realized. On May 1st, 1950, the Central Office moved from

Pimlico to Portman Square, and there, at No. 27, Temple House was established. Pimlico had represented the decaying architecture of a miscalculating Victorian speculative builder. Portman Square was part of the glory of Georgian London. 'Bus routes and underground stations clustered round it, but not quite near enough to menace its residential dignity. The rooms of No. 27 were spacious and beautifully proportioned. Built for an age of elegance it had eluded the latter-day business enterprise which turned the east side of the square into an outpost of London's Oxford Street shopping centre and the north side into a twentieth-century rabbit-warren where luxury-flat dwellers ascended in electric lifts to constricted and featureless habitations.

It was, perhaps, a little hard that Ernest Green's retirement coincided almost precisely with the move which he had done so much to bring about. Since 1934 he had served the W.E.A. as General Secretary. In fact he had served in much the same capacity for five years before that, since as assistant secretary his term of office had covered the tragic mortal illness of Muir and the collapse of Firth. If ever a man deserved compensation for the penury of Pimlico it was Ernest Green. He found it in continued service as an honorary officer, or rather as two honorary officers: as honorary treasurer in succession to J. J. Mallon, who retired in the same year, and as president of the International Federation of W.E.A.s, which had always been a major concern to him.

Nineteen-fifty was altogether a year of change. J. J. Mallon retired from the treasurership: without him financial crises would take on a new appearance of austerity. R. H. Tawney retired from his vice-presidency; the writing of economic history reclaimed him. Up in Yorkshire Ezra Fisher retired from his district secretaryship. South Yorkshire would miss his energy and his experience, indeed it was called upon to do so, for he did not long survive retirement. Nor, indeed, did E. S. Cartwright. Meetings of the Central Council seemed strange without them.

So with a new headquarters office came new men, or old men in a new capacity. Harry Nutt sat in the chair of Ernest Green as General Secretary, and W. C. E. Gregory, a newcomer to the Central Office, though not to the W.E.A., succeeded Harry Nutt as organizing secretary with a special care for the trade-union connection. He brought a rich and varied experience to the job, W.E.A. student, Cambridge graduate, one-time member of the Iron and Steel Trades Confederation, he knew the ground he had to cultivate. The *Highway*, too, experienced changes. From a seven-months' issue it had moved hopefully in 1947 to an "all-the-year-round" issue under the auspices of Edmund Poole, its war-time editor having abandoned it a year earlier. As such it proved an unduly expensive luxury; so in 1949 it reverted to type and J. Hampden Jackson of the Cambridge Board of Extra-Mural Studies shouldered its editorship, thus relieving its profit and loss account of a salary charge arising from its absorption of Edmund Poole's time.

With all this change there were, happily, elements of personal continuity. Year in year out Horace Nobbs of the Union of Post Office Workers, a pioneer of W.E.T.U.C. activity in the years between the wars, continued to preside over the Standing Orders Committee at successive annual conferences. It is probable that few services to the W.E.A. combine so large a measure of worry with so small a crown of glory, and the W.E.A. will doubtless not realize how much it relies on his mastery of points of order until at some far-distant date it has to do without him. Meanwhile, Miss Casey, starting as a clerk at the age of fourteen plus, having served the clerical work of the Central Office through four changes of General Secretary and three changes of location, remained at her post. By conventional standards it is considered unseemly to refer to a lady's length of days, and if Miss Casey really showed signs of advancing age it would doubtless be ill-mannered to call attention to her thirty years or so of service to the W.E.A. But outgoing officers know what they owe to her devotion, and incoming officers know what they owe to her experience.

Thus supported, the W.E.A. enters upon its fiftieth year. In so far as statistics can tell a story, and admittedly they cannot tell a whole story, the going has been good, with ups and downs, during these difficult post-war years. Branch membership, which stood at 37,159 in May 1945, had fallen to 30,441 in 1952, though the number of branches had risen from 876 to

1,006. District membership, which stood at 5,424 in 1945, was 4,187 in 1952, and 2,660 affiliated societies in 1945 had risen to 2,809 in 1952. But branch membership continued as ever to lag behind class membership, which suggests the perpetuation in some quarters of a belief that, in spite of an authoritative pronouncement to the contrary, it is better to receive than to give. The really significant figure, however, since quality education continues to be the peculiar concern of the W.E.A., is that which concerns the university tutorial classes. By the session 1948–49 the tutorial classes were approaching their pre-war strength with a total of 889—they constituted something approaching 14 per cent of all classes. In 1953 there were 987 tutorial classes and less exacting classes on a scale comparable with that of previous years.

There they stand, the figures that mark the progress of a great movement. But do they? We know something of student numbers, but what do we know of student quality? Not as much as we should like.

We know that the proportion of manual workers has fallen: in some areas, in the Home Counties for example, classes appear to consist largely of the class for which the pioneer University Extension Lectures catered, men and women who would not, in 1903, have been described as "workers". But precisely how far this change reflects changes in the whole industrial and class structure of Great Britain it is difficult to calculate.

We know that the universities supply a growing army of tutors and that their academic qualifications are impeccable. We do not know how far these tutors represent, as they once did, the missionary zeal of university staffs carrying their riches outside the walls to a working class starved of cultural and intellectual life, how far they consist of young men and women seeking an interesting career (as they have every right to do) or an addition to their regular income (which they have every reason to need) in a field less exacting and routine-ridden than school-teaching.

We know that the universities are playing a much larger part in the provision of classes, encouraged by the existing grant regulations, and by the spectacular expansion in university departments made possible by post-war government policy. We do not know whether they are incurring responsibility for work of sub-university standard and whether the W.E.A. has managed to work out the proper line of demarcation between their work and its own. S. G. Raybould, of Leeds University, whose experience of W.E.A. activities is equalled by his knowledge of how university extra-mural departments actually work, has expressed doubts on this matter which have been the subject of keen controversial discussion since he raised the question in 1950.[1]

We know that numbers of classes and numbers in classes keep up; but we cannot be sure that the intellectual quality of those who attend them is what it was in the days of the pioneers. Have we the same chance today of finding a Price or a Wadsworth, a Cartwright or a Tomlinson, among a group of W.E.A. students? And if not, is it because human quality or human resolution is failing, or for the happier reason that the educational opportunities for which the W.E.A. has worked now carry the Prices and the Wadsworths, the Cartwrights and the Tomlinsons, via free secondary grammar-school education straight to the universities and the liberal professions for which their natural abilities fit them?

All of which means that the interpretation of our bare figures must have reference to what is happening outside the arena of W.E.A. activities as well as what is happening inside it. And to the changing class structure, the prodigious widening of educational opportunity, and the expansion of university departments, we must add yet another conditioning factor, perhaps the most potent of the lot: the B.B.C.

> Be not afeard; the isle is full of noises,
> Sounds, and sweet airs, that give delight, and hurt not.

So Caliban was able to assure newcomers to the Island of the *Tempest*. But can we be so certain that it is true of our own island? We have so far been spared the dangers of commercial radio with its consignment of programmes to advertising agencies operating with the oblique object of attracting listening

[1] See *The English Universities and Adult Education*, by S. G. Raybould; Workers' Educational Association, 1951.

audiences for advertised goods, though Mr. Churchill's Government has now opened a door to its introduction in the field of television. But so far the B.B.C. has been allowed exclusive control of the air and has exercised its power with commendable regard for the provision of educative material and the development of qualitative appreciation. In the early days of its activities between the wars it was noticeable that audiences for single lectures were not readily forthcoming. This is understandable in an age when the voices of all the most eminent experts of literature, art, science, philosophy and economics can be heard round the domestic hearth. Nor is it to be deplored so long as the B.B.C. is permitted to rule the air and does so with the profound sense of responsibility for public service which it exhibits today. But there remains the danger that the very luxuriance of what is provided may encourage the habit of *half-listening*. The B.B.C. caters for a public naturally disinclined to engage in any effort of mental concentration and unaware of the qualitative satisfaction which results from comprehending the plan of a whole symphony, play, lecture, as the case may be, instead of bits here and there which attract effortless attention. A population of satisfied *half-listeners* is not likely to provide a good field for the kind of adult education which demands continuous attention and active response.

It may therefore happen that the historian who celebrates the W.E.A.'s centenary will look upon its statistics with somewhat different eyes, measuring success not by the growth of student numbers, but by their diminution. If this is so it will be because the Association has pursued its second half-century in the light of valedictory advice which R. H. Tawney offered as it neared the completion of its first. The W.E.A. has, he said, two "pillars": its "working-class foundations" and "the solidity and genuineness of its work". If it is to preserve both, it must not be led into "providing education for those who can most easily be induced to undertake it" instead of "for those who need it most". He added that a condition for the acceptance of such education was "self-discipline and effort".

What did Albert Mansbridge think of this fifty-year-old offspring of his early genius, with its army of tutors, its potent influence in the educational world, its mounting membership, its stream of expert publications, and its spacious headquarters in Portman Square, W.I? We cannot know, since he died at his home on the Devon coast a year before the jubilee celebration in which he would surely have expressed his views. But from what he said and wrote in later life it is clear that he was well satisfied with the harvest he had sown and confident of its sustaining value to those who reaped it. As far as he was concerned there was peculiar relevance in words from the Book of Proverbs which were sung as an anthem at his memorial service on November 12th, 1952:

> Happy is the man that findeth wisdom,
> And the man that getteth understanding.

> *       *       *

> Her ways are ways of pleasantness,
> And all her paths are peace.

To those who are left to solve the problems which complicate W.E.A. policy as it enters upon its second half-century it may at times appear that not *all* her paths are peace. And to the tutor who sets out at nightfall across an icebound shoulder of the Pennines or through the murk of a November fog on country roads, it may sometimes seem that her ways are not always ways of pleasantness. One should, however, read a little further in this same Book of Proverbs and take comfort from the assurance that:

> The wise shall inherit glory:
> But shame shall be the promotion of fools.

GEORGE ALLEN & UNWIN LTD
LONDON: 40 MUSEUM STREET, W.C.1
CAPE TOWN: 58-60 LONG STREET
SYDNEY, N.S.W.: 55 YORK STREET
TORONTO: 91 WELLINGTON STREET WEST
CALCUTTA: 17 CENTRAL AVE., P.O. DHARAMTALA
BOMBAY: 15 GRAHAM ROAD, BALLARD ESTATE
WELLINGTON, N.Z.: 8 KINGS CRESCENT, LOWER HUTT